THE LEGEND OF OLD STONE RANCH

JOHN WORTH CLOUD

36579

Published in Fandangleland and
Distributed by J. W. Cloud
Albany, Texas 76430

Second Printing

Terrill Wheeler Printing Co.
Denton, Texas

For *Birdie, George, and Maxine*
WITH MY LOVE AND GRATITUDE

Foreword

Many Historians have noted the extraordinary speed with which the western prairies of Texas changed from the wild frontier of the buffalo to the docile rangeland of the Hereford. The leap from Stone Age simplicity to Twentieth Century complexity was accomplished within the span of a single generation — and was so successful that the men who made the leap were, most of them, unaware that their accomplishment was an historical rarity. Wholly dedicated to action, absorbed by each day's business, they retained little remembrance of the steps by which they climbed from adventurous pioneer to settled old timer.

Today in West Texas we are trying to preserve and mark as historically important the structures they built and then abandoned as nomadic inclinations moved them elsewhere. We are trying to gather into museums samples of the articles of living which they vigorously used and then cast aside as better articles became available to them. We have discovered that their brief age — the Old West — seems to have endless fascination for numerous and varied people from other parts of the nation, and we seek to interest those people by perpetuating cowboy dress, by re-creating frontier towns, by holding festivals which commemorate the pioneer spirit.

In need of equal attention, if the period is to be preserved properly, is careful research of the life histories of the men and women who lived in the era. Newton Givens, whose story is recorded in this book, was a prototype of the breed, and John Worth Cloud has chosen a worthy protagonist for the work which follows this introduction. If we can understand the nature and motives of a man like Givens, we can have a true concept of how a pristine stretch of the American continent could be completely made over in less than half a century.

Mr. Cloud decided that all the elements of Givens' life tended to poetic interpretation. Rather than record the Givens story in prose form of customary history, he has hoped that writing it in verse will enlarge and illuminate our perception of such a highly unusual man and his times.

Mr. Cloud's able and commendable work is a bold experiment and deserves our attention as a refreshing and innovative method of making our West Texas heritage live anew.

—*John Ben Shepperd*

PAST PRESIDENT
TEXAS STATE HISTORICAL SURVEY
COMMITTEE
AND
TEXAS HISTORICAL FOUNDATION

Odessa, Texas

Contents

Contents

Preface

I Have Been interested
in history and writing most of my adult life. Until
1950, except for some published short stories and
poems, my writing was confined to various news-
paper areas, and radio script. During the years I
owned and operated a country publishing plant and
edited my own newspapers at Huntington in the
East Texas piney woods, an enviable amount of recognition for editorial, feature, and ad writing came
my way.

It was not until sometime after 1953, when Jo
and I moved to Albany, that I became interested in
literary writing. My oil business demanded consider-
able travel and the rugged grandeur of this area
deeply appealed to me. Here the Comanche and buffalo could almost be seen disappearing into the horizon. The rich cultural heritage was being reproduced
in the Fort Griffin Fandangle. Every old-timer had
his bit of history to share. Here was history with a
gripping new dimension.

Newton Givens and Old Stone Ranch came alive
following a delightful visit to the Putnam Ranch

and a tour of various sites pertinent to the story. Extensive research followed. *The Legend* took shape and like Topsy, "it just grew." The love story of Newton and Lucinda is fiction but the rest was written after diligent inquiry and investigation. I am indebted to many people for interviews, factual material, and historical data. Throughout the lengthy period of writing and revision, I was fortunate to be married to a good typist and an understanding critic.

Writing *The Legend* in verse was an irresistible challenge. While researching *Shackelford County Sketches* by Don Biggers, I was so impressed by the grave scene that I wrote it in verse (Elegy, p. 383). That started it! Once the feel of its natural rhythm became familiar, it was almost like writing prose. From the beginning I was told that a long narrative poem would go unread . . . but how else does one deal with a challenge that is bigger than he? It is sincerely hoped that you will enjoy reading it as much as I enjoyed writing it.

The fact that a publisher could not be found for the book resulted in printing it myself in the shop of *The Albany News.* I am most grateful to Mr. and Mrs. John McGaughey for the use of their equipment, to my daughter, Mrs. Maxine Dudley, for doing the press work, and to Mrs. C. for doing the proofreading.—JWC.

By: Ratliff

SENATE CONCURRENT RESOLUTION NO. 8

WHEREAS, The history of Texas and the men who made it, coupled with the legend and drama of the frontier, have been captured by John Worth Cloud in his saga of Texas borderlands, THE LEGEND OF OLD STONE RANCH; and _____

WHEREAS, An epic poem of Texas ranking with the famed KALEVALA, the national epic poem of Finland, THE LEGEND OF THE OLD STONE RANCH is a collection of colorful episodes from Texas history written in unrhymed alliterative eight-syllabled verse telling a story, like the KALEVALA, of a specific geographical area; and _____

WHEREAS, Mr. Cloud's poetic interpretation of early 19th century life on the Texas frontier involves the reader in the fictional romance of Newton Givens and his beloved Lucinda against the backdrop of rugged grandeur that characterizes Shackelford County, where Comanche and buffalo can almost be seen today disappearing into the horizon; and _____

WHEREAS, In discussing the book, the poet said: "Newton Givens and Old Stone Ranch came alive (to me) following a delightful visit to the Putnam Ranch and a tour of various sites pertinent to the story . . ."; and _____

WHEREAS, While the main characters in the book are fiction, events surrounding their lives were very much a part of everyday life on the frontier, and the story was written only after diligent inquiry and investigation; and _____

WHEREAS, Mr. Cloud said that writing the legend in verse was an irresistable challenge, one that reached him while he was researching "Shackelford County Sketches" by Don Biggers, when the grave scene so impressed him that he wrote it in verse: _____

". . . On a high hill overlooking
Old Stone Ranch, a cemetery
With a single grave stands vigil
Oversweeping, rugged grandeur
Of a land now roamed by cattle.

The discovery, inadvertent
Of the tomb was made by persons
Looking for long-buried treasure.
In the tiny hand-hewn casket
Was the body of an infant.

Rocks and hills hold fast the secret
Of the tender hands that placed it
In the hallowed earth to slumber.

Yet, to one's imagination
Comes the vision of a woman,
Bowed in grief by her bereavement,
Raising tear-dimmed eyes to heaven,

Asking God to grant her surcease
From the sorrow in her bosom . . ."; and _____

1

WHEREAS, On June 20, 1969, the Texas Historical Survey Committee gave to John Worth Cloud of Albany, Texas, the official state award for "Best Historical Publication of the Year on Local or Regional History" in recognition of his book, LEGEND OF OLD STONE RANCH; and

WHEREAS, It is appropriate that the 61st Legislature, 1st Called Session of the State of Texas commend John Worth Cloud for his distinguished accomplishment in delineating the glorious country that is Texas and interlacing romance and description with the charming legends of American Indians to make THE LEGEND OF OLD STONE RANCH a true Texas saga; now, therefore, be it

RESOLVED, By the Senate of the 61st Legislature, 1st Called Session, the House of Representatives concurring, that the Texas Legislature hereby congratulate John Worth Cloud on his momentous work, THE LEGEND OF OLD STONE RANCH, and with this Resolution officially designate the saga of the Texas frontier as the official epic poem of Texas; and, be it further

RESOLVED, That copies of this Resolution be prepared for John Worth Cloud of Albany, Texas, for the Texas State Historical Survey Committee, and for the Archives Division, Texas State Library, in expressing the will of the Texas Legislature that THE LEGEND OF OLD STONE RANCH be the official epic poem of Texas.

_____
Lieutenant Governor

_____
Speaker of the House

I hereby certify that S. C. R. No. 8 was adopted by the Senate on August 5, 1969.

_____
Secretary of the Senate

I hereby certify that S. C. R. No. 8 was adopted by the House on August 6, 1969.

_____
Chief Clerk of the House

2

THE
LEGEND
OF
OLD
STONE
RANCH

Prologue

IN A LAND of rugged grandeur
In Throckmorton County, Texas,
Near the sprawling ranch headquarters
Of the J. A. Matthews family,
Lie the mouldering massive ruins
Of the first ranch ever settled
In the valley of the Clear Fork
Of the wayward Brazos River.

Secrets of the past surround it
With a mantle of enchantment.
In the litter and the rubble,
Never knowing fond fulfillment,
Lie the dreams of Newton Givens
And his lovely wife Lucinda:
Dreams that tragedy has trampled
In the dust of dying decades.

When the ranch came into being
In the middle Eighteen Fifties,
It was well within the borders
Of the dread *Comancheria*—
Land of ruthless, warring Indians.

Tumbled ruins are reminiscent
Of the vibrant, yet chaotic,
Times that changed the Clear Fork Country
From a glorious primeval

The Legend of Old Stone Ranch

Realm of buffaloes and Indians
Into a majestic ranchland.

Born of native stone and mortar,
Cut and mixed by master craftsmen,
Like a citadel constructed
To withstand the fearful onslaught
Of the fierce Comanche raiders,
The ranch boasted many comforts
Known to homes of wealth and plenty
In the far-off cultured regions
Long inhabited by white men.

Early settlers of the country,
Those who followed in the footsteps
Of the rancher when the Civil
War was ended and the Indians
Had been driven, for the most part,
Farther westward toward their stronghold
In the Palo Duro Canyon,
Aptly named the spreading acres
Old Stone Ranch, as all the buildings
And the huge corrals for livestock
Were of weathered limestone fashioned.

What the founder called his holdings
Is a mystery long buried
In the tomb of Captain Givens,
Who himself was an enigma
Poised upon the swift transition
Of an era spawning many
Baffling, weird extravaganzas
Destined to remain unfathomed.

Chapter One

English Rebel

NEWTON GIVENS was a member
Of the legion born to wander:
Men to whom far, distant pastures
Always look a little greener;
Restless men who lack resistance
To the call of bold adventure.
He was born in London, England,
In the early Eighteen Hundreds.
Rebel son of wealthy parents,
Givens ran away from Oxford
To explore the world in answer
To a driving urge that sent him
On a journey that extended
Over continents and oceans
To the mystic lands forbidden
All except that mystic army
Fortune chooses for her soldiers.
Henry Givens, Newton's father,
Was an English shipping baron;
Owned a fleet of large four-masted
Ships which netted him a fortune.

Keen of intellect, young Givens
Early learned to value money,
Knew the comforts it afforded
And the pleasures it could purchase.
Too, he had appreciation
For the art of gracious living;
Liked to hunt and had a passion
For thoroughbreds, both in horses
And the hounds that claimed the trophies
In the ancient sports of England.

He had learned in school that lending
Money to his spendthrift classmates,
For short terms at rates of interest
That would stagger money lenders
In staid London banking circles,
Added up in pounds and shillings,
Swelling the allowance given
Him by proud and doting parents.

II

At the outset of his travels,
Bound by motives mercenary,
He had made a resolution
To apply his knack for gambling,
Which returned him handsome profits,
And to keep his sharp eyes open
For advantages that offered
Opportunity to better
His financial situation.

At the time of his departure
From the foggy shores of England,
Givens was a striking figure
And attracted quick attention
From the people he encountered.
Tall and pleasant, with wide shoulders
That bespoke the tireless muscles
Rippling through his sturdy body,
He was quick to win the friendship
Of the strangers, men and women,
That he thought might serve his purpose
In the business and the pleasure
Of fulfilling his ambitions.

His were blue-grey eyes that twinkled
In the warmth of conversation
When the stream of life ran smoothly,
But could change in half an instant
To a depth of penetration
That could fathom inmost secrets
Of a man and leave him trembling
In the knowledge he was naked
At the bar of piercing reason.
Unpredictable, erratic,
He possessed the will to conquer
Heights that others would not tackle.

III

After several years of roving,
Newton found his spirit flagging,
Felt that he had seen the wonders
Of the world which first impelled him
To forsake the halls of Oxford.

5

He was sick of the abysmal
Way of living that existed
On the ships that he had captained:
Overloading, undermanning,
Overcrowding, underfeeding,
And the lashings, which were common,
Had become to him repulsive—
Great reforms were in the making.
He had made a tidy fortune,
But he doubted it was worth it.

He recalled the dazzling beauty
Of the temples and pagodas
Of a dozen eastern countries.
He remembered, too, cathedrals,
Saintly shrines and humble churches
From the Holy Land to Burma,
That aroused, at times, deep longings
Which he stifled lest they sway him
From .his lusty way of living—
He would contemplate them later.

IV

In Quebec where he unloaded
Silks and spices from the Far East
When the wanderlust that plagued him
Lost its keen edge, he decided
In the early Eighteen Forties
On a trip to Massachusetts
To the shipyards of the builders
Of the new, swift Yankee Clipper.

He would sail in style to England
For a visit with his parents.

While awaiting the delivery
Of his ship in Boston, Givens
Suddenly came face to face with
An old friend of his from Oxford.
It was from his former classmate
That he learned his aging mother
Had been dead three years, a victim
Of stark loneliness and heartbreak.
And his father, shortly after,
Had been killed in a disaster
Off the coast of Asia Minor.

The Givens family lawyer,
Who had searched in vain for Newton,
Would be happy to receive him;
His inheritance was waiting
In the sturdy Bank of England.

V

It was two days after Christmas
When young Givens sailed for London,
Dreading the details awaiting
His attention in arranging
Settlement of legal matters.
He considered disposition
Of the estate his parents left him:
Should or should he not accept it?
Long he pondered its disposal.

In the end the humbled **Givens**,
As a token of affection
To the memory of his elders,
Gave two-thirds of it to further
Causes of the Church of England.
When his business was completed,
He set sail for sunny Venice,
Seeking respite from the torture
Of his conscience for the suffering
He had brought upon his parents . . .

In the Palace of the Doges
He found comfort in the marvels
Of the Sixteenth-century artists.
And he found fresh inspiration
In the fine mosaics patterned
On the walls of the cathedral
Of St. Mark. And there, while feeding
Pigeons in the ancient churchyard,
He fell into conversation
With an understanding *padri*.

VI

After Newton had unburdened
His heart to the kindly father,
Told him how the grief he suffered
Through the treatment of his parents
Almost came alive to taunt him,
Like Pygmalion's Galatea,
He asked for advice and counsel.
Said the wise and saintly *padri*:

"In America are golden
Opportunities for young men.
Take your wealth and youth and knowledge
To this great land and apply them
In the manner God intended.
You will find, perchance, the answers
To the problems that beset you.
Time will heal your wounds and heartaches,
Make you strong again and eager
For the journey on the highroad
Toward the sunlit hills where travelers
See afar and find true joy in
Bringing happiness to others."

Chapter Two

Crescent City Carnival

ROUNDING UP his crew, the chastened
Rover turned his speedy Clipper
Toward New Orleans, determined
To amend his way of living.

Two years since, in distant Hong Kong,
Newton had been well acquainted
With a man named Edwin Lovelace
From New Orleans. Now he wondered
If, by chance, his friend would be there.

When he reached the Crescent City,
Carnival was in full blossom.
He could feel the joyous spirit
Of the crowds that watched the splendors
Of the fete unroll before them.

Lonely in the festive city,
Givens learned upon inquiry
That there was a Lovelace family,
Well-to-do and well-respected,
Living in a Creole mansion
On the Avenue St. Charles.

Calling at the address given
He was warmly and sincerely
Welcomed by his old friend's family.
There had been no word from Edwin
In a year, but he had mentioned
Givens many times in letters,
Always speaking highly of him . . .

Malcolm Lovelace, Edwin's father,
Was a colonel in the army,
And his mother was a cheerful
Lady of the French South, daughter
Of aristocratic planters.
Other members of the household
Were three daughters, Annette, Nanette—
Twins who showed their Creole blood line,
Sparkling, full of fun, vivacious—
And their opposite, Lucinda,
Fair and Titian-tressed, retiring,
Sensitive and with a gentle
Bent toward depth and the religious
Leanings of her Pilgrim forebears.
Uncle Jacque and Grand-Mere DuPuy
Spent the winters in the town house,
But in early spring departed
For The Oaks, a pet name given
To their Natchez-Trace plantation.

As a servant brought in coffee,
Thick and black, a Creole mixture,
Happy laughter from the staircase
Heralded the coming bevy:
Gay young beauties, Lovelace sisters

And their friends, some half a dozen,
Who had been upstairs for fittings
Of the gorgeous gowns the seamstress
Was completing for the gala
Ball of Carnival and romance.

Following the introductions,
And a demitasse of coffee,
All the girls except Lucinda
Traipsed outside into the garden
"To enjoy the sun," they hinted,
But in truth they all were anxious
To discuss the handsome stranger.

II

Colonel Lovelace was insistent
That this charming friend of Edwin's
Be their guest while in the city.
Thinking back on his aloneness,
And a subtle Mona-Lisa
Smile free-given by Lucinda,
Newton fell into agreement.
After lunch a coachman took him
To the harbor in a carriage.
In addition to his clothing,
He picked up a chest of treasures,
Rare mememtoes of his travels,
From which he could make selections
To convey appreciation
To his gracious benefactors.

Colonel Lovelace helped young Givens
With his baggage to a guest room
Which looked down upon the courtyard
Where banana plants and bamboo
Grew around a crystal fountain.

Walking over to the window,
He gazed downward through the shadows
Of the evening as they deepened,
And a strange nostalgic yearning
Welled within his inner being:
A nostalgia for something
He had never known — a feeling
Of attraction to a woman.

Up until the present moment,
He had always been the center
Of attraction to the fair sex.
He had played the field, enjoyed it—
His had been the pick for asking.
With the turning of the table,
He was shaken and bewildered.

III

On the morrow Colonel Lovelace
Planned to show his guest the city . . .

As they drove along admiring
Different types of architecture—
French and Spanish and the blendings
Of the two — the colonel pointed
Out the sights he thought would interest

His attentive young companion.
"There's the Place d'Armes," he told him,
"Where much of the thrilling history
Of New Orleans was written.

Through the Vieux Carre, French Quarter,
They continued their excursion
To Canal Street and the section
Where the business and the commerce
Of the bustling city flourished.
On they went past staid cathedrals,
Statues, parks, and lovely gardens,
Where exotic plants and flowers
Of the semi-tropic region
Grew in rank and wild profusion.
Visiting the old French Market
With its scarred arcades and pillars,
Newton smelled the mingled odors:
Garden produce, fruit and sea food;
Heard the vendors haggling prices
With the frugal Creole matrons.
It was strangely reminiscent
Of the Oriental markets
He had visited on his journeys.
For a haunting, fleeting moment
He was homesick, bothered, restless:
Was the siren voice demanding
A renewal of allegiance?

In the market place some Indians
Dressed in native garb were selling
Silverware and other handcraft.
Newton watched them, fascinated.

He observed the resignation
Stamped upon their passive faces.
Were these poor and wretched creatures
Specimens of noble red men?

An authority on Indians,
Colonel Lovelace answered questions
Fired at him in rapid order.
He was much surprised that Givens
Could express such avid interest
In the Indians' tribal cultures
And their struggle for existence.

IV

On the way home, Newton queried:
How did Mardi Gras get started
In New Orleans? I attended
One in Paris, when a towhead,
With my parents. It was something
That I always shall remember!"

"Mardi Gras in Louisiana,"
Colonel Lovelace told his listener,
"Started long ago when weary
Iberville and his tired troopers
Rested by a stream of water:
Sixteen Ninety-nine, Shrove Tuesday,
Found his homesick men remembering
That in France grand celebrations
Of the ancient date were starting.
Labeled, in commemoration,
Bayou Mardi Gras, the little

Stream was soon to see the founding
Of a settlement . . . and townsmen
Celebrated Mardi Gras with
True Old-World enthusiasm.

"Seventeen Seventy-six found
Mardi Gras a well established
Custom in the Crescent City.
When Ulloa took New Orleans
Over for Spain, he suppressed it
On the ground that street-cavorting
In masked costumes was conducive
To crime — if not insurrection!
It was soon revived, however,
By infuriated Frenchmen.

"By the middle Eighteen Twenties,
Narrow streets of the French Quarter
Were the scene of gay processions
Heralding the first parading
Of the great festive occasion.

"Twelfth night balls, *Bals du roi*,
Starting sixth of January,
Usher in a gala season
Of masquerade balls that continue
With subscription balls and soirees
Until Mardi Gras, Shrove Tuesday.

"Seven years ago young Creoles
Went to great expense to present
The first pageant of importance:
Vans, superbly ornamented,

Richly decorated horses,
Bands of music, personation
Of heroes, cavaliers, and figures
From mythology and history
Were displayed in showy splendor.

"Since that time expense and effort
Have enhanced the presentations.
This year's Mardi Gras will feature
A torchlit parade . . . the first one.
Floats with allegoric figures
Will be added and paraders
Promise New Orleans a pageant
Staggering imagination!

"There will be tableaux presented
At the opera house preceding
The ball. Happy masqueraders
Will be dressed in finest costumes
Ever seen in Crescent City.
Yes, Mardi Gras this year will be
A spectacular occasion."

V

. . . Carnival was nearly over,
The grand ball and gay Fat Tuesday—
Mardi Gras, the grand finale—
Were among remaining features,
When the colonel received orders
To report posthaste for duty
At a frontier fort in distant

Territory of the Indians.
There was mounting redskin trouble
And his presence was most urgent.

While preparing for his journey
To the far-off, frenzied frontier,
Colonel Lovelace talked with Newton,
Asked him to fulfill a promise
He had made to take his family
To the ball, which would be held in
The new opera house located
In the Vieux Carre. The costume
He had chosen was a perfect
Fit for Newton, whose reluctance
Was overshadowed by the challenge
To play role of fond attendant
To so charming an entourage.

VI

"It is customary practice,"
Said the colonel to his proxy,
"To present one's call-out partners
At the festive ball a favor.
Here are those that I selected
For the girls and Madame Lovelace."

It was then that Newton asked him:
"Sir, may I, with your permission,
Also give the girls a token
Of esteem? It is a pleasure
I have planned since the acceptance
Of the invitation given
Me to be your guest of honor."

. . . At a small bazaar in Bangkok—
"Market of the Thieves" they call it,
In the Nakorn Kasem section—
He had found a silver bracelet
With inlaid designs so clever
He could not resist its purchase.
As he handed it to Nannette,
Grand-Mere DuPuy beamed approval.

From a Moor in distant Dakar
He had bought a fan of ivory:
Beautiful and ornamental
As well as practical and useful.
This was for Annette. She hugged him!
Her exuberance was boundless.

Last he stood before Lucinda,
And his hand was trembling as he
Handed her a brilliant necklace.
'Twas an heirloom rare and ancient
From a maharaja's palace.
He had won it playing poker
With the monarch's black-sheep grandson
In Calcutta's famed casino.
From a slender strand of braided
Gold so delicate it almost
Seemed transparent, dangled figures
Representing Brahma, Vishnu,
Shiva—sacred Hindu Triad.
And the image of Pushkara—
Tiny, detailed, and exquisite—
Formed a clasp of sparkling beauty.

As she caught her breath in wonder
At the splendor of the present,
And was hesitant to take it,
He became abashed and murmured:
"Won't you please, my dear, accept it
In the spirit it is offered?"
At a slight nod from her mother,
Lucinda took the gift in silence.

VII

In the evening neighbors started
Gathering in the Lovelace parlor.
Madame Lovelace had invited
Them to share the upper gallery
Where the first of torchlit pageants
Could be viewed in ease and comfort.

Not long after they assembled
Bands and maskers started pouring
Down the avenue in numbers
That amazed the guest from England.

Negro slaves made capering escorts
For the entries as they carried
Out the themes of Creole sponsors.
Dressed in white, the glistening darkies
Held aloft their reddish flambeaux,
Casting garish glows of orange
Softly over gay paraders.

There were varied types of entries
In the beautiful procession.
One huge float, the Court of Neptune,

Topped the others in its splendor:
Gorgeous costumes were a-glitter
With a myriad of jewels
Shining like the fins of fishes
From the depths of Neptune's kingdom.
Crowds of merry, mirthful people,
Shouting, laughing, and applauding,
Lined the banquettes on the edges
Of the avenue and struggled
Merrily for treasured favors
Flung from carriages by riders.

As he watched in rapt attention,
Listening to the explanation
By his hostess of traditions
On which Carnival was founded,
Givens knew he liked this country—
Liked the people who befriended
Him and made him feel so welcome.

VIII

. . . By the time the Lovelace party
Made its entrance in the lobby,
Other guests with invitations
Were presenting them for checking
With a master file. Imposters
Had been known to take advantage
Of by-hook-or-crook admission.
The Lovelaces were welcomed. They
Made a gay, impressive entrance.
Many eyes were turned upon them
As they gracefully ascended

The double staircase to the loge
Which had been assigned their party.

As the house lights dimmed and footlights
Announced the parting of the curtains,
The huge audience was silenced
For a solitary moment.
Then applause reverberated
As the first tableau presented
Olden court of Cleopatra
In a burst of dazzling beauty.
Other tableaux quickly followed,
Each more colorful and striking
Than its glowing predecessor.

When preliminaries ended
And the house lights fluttered softly,
Men in masks of many patterns
Gathered on the floor below them.
As the revelry proceeded,
Maskers in elaborate costumes
Looked about them for their ladies.

Breathlessly the girls awaited,
Hoping their names would be chosen.
With each passing, thrilling moment
Their excitement grew to bursting.
Then at last they heard a call-out:
"Mademoiselle Nannette Lovelace!"
Uncle Jacque, with gallant gesture,
Drew her chair back and accompanied
Her downstairs to a committee
Member who in turn escorted
Her in safety to her partner.

When Annette received her call-out
The procedure was repeated.
Off she whirled in graceful rhythm
In the arms of a gold-turbaned,
Gayly costumed Eastern sultan.

IX

Last, Lucinda's name resounded
Through the ballroom, and she curtsied
As she met the gallant Givens.
Tenderly his arm encircled
Her and she was dimly conscious
Of the mystery surrounding
Him tonight as on they glided
To the lilting strains of magic
In a waltz from old Vienna.

While they whirled in perfect cadence,
Oblivious of other dancers,
Newton brushed her Titian tresses
With a kiss and softly whispered:
"Ah, my darling, my Lucinda,
Would this waltz could last forever!"

Eyes downcast, and with the tracery
Of a smile, she gently answered:
"Truly, my own thoughts you utter."

It was three o'clock when Grand-Mere
Intimated she was tiring.
Overriding mumbled protests
Of the others, Madame Lovelace
Had the coachman bring the carriage.

X

When they reached home, Newton, restless,
Walked into the moonlit courtyard.
He approached the crystal fountain,
Sat upon its edge and pondered
All the things that had befallen
Him since reaching Crescent City.

As the moonbeams skimmed the water,
He was calmed and fell to musing:
"Why should it have been Lucinda
I would fall in love with? Truly,
Even though, somehow, I win her,
I would always feel unworthy
Of such heavenly perfection.
Only in this southern household
With its constant chaperonage
Could such innocence be nurtured . . .
She is all a man could hope for:
Tender, lovely, intellectual,
Yet she is naive and forthright,
Unaffected, natural, honest . . . "

Lost in reverie, he never
Heard the soft approaching footsteps.
Suddenly she was beside him:
"Dearest, I could not sleep either,
And I came into the garden,
Knowing in my heart you'd be here."
As the moon was disappearing
In the west, he asked her simply:
"Will you marry me, Lucinda?"

"Yes, but you must ask my papa."

After breakfast Newton counseled
With the elders of the family.
He began by stating frankly
He was in love with Lucinda;
Told them also of the early
Morning tryst within the garden.
"Of course, under circumstances,"
He informed them, "I no longer
Can remain your guest." He wondered
Just how long the absent colonel
Would be gone upon his campaign.
Mrs. Lovelace here related
How, when he was a lieutenant,
He had left her for a fortnight
And was two years in returning.
Time elapse, of course, depended
On the outcome of his mission.

Chapter Three

Momentous Decision

FOLLOWING their conversation
Newton told them he was going
To Fort Washita forthwith and
Ask Lucinda's hand in marriage.
Uncle Jaque advised against it:
Said the country was too dangerous;
Stated it would be much better
To engage in correspondence.
Adamant in his conviction,
Newton told them he was leaving
As soon as he could sell the Clipper . . .

The demand for Yankee Clippers
Made it possible for Givens
To transact the business quickly.
And he earned a tidy bonus.

Grand-Mere DuPuy, quick to sanction
Newton's purpose and intentions,
Said that it was time to return
To The Oaks, and she invited
Him to join them on that portion
Of the trip that lay directly
On his route to Indian country.

On the riverboat to Natchez
Givens marvelled at the beauty
Of the country. The plantations
Seemed alive with slaves engaging
In details of cotton raising.
The palatial homes impressed him,
And his hostess was ingenious
In relating the traditions
Of the South and of the gracious
Living enjoyed by the planters.

. . . Natchez was a wild port city,
Murder, gambling, prostitution,
And intrigue ran free, unbridled,
Like its bustling, booming commerce.

II

At the livery stable, Newton
Looked with eyes of earnest longing
At the thoroughbred the DuPuys
Had brought with them as an extra
From their famed plantation paddock.
Uncle Jacque and Grand-Mere DuPuy,
Noting his keen admiration
Of the animal, named Beauty,
Were quite firm in their insistence
That he take it as a parting
Token of their sincere wishes
For a safe and speedy journey.
For a pack horse they suggested
That he buy a sturdy gelding
Offered by the stable owner . . .

North of town their roads divided.
Up the Natchez Trace the DuPuys
Traveled toward The Oaks in silence.
Louisiana, to the westward,
Over the wide Mississippi,
Beckoned Newton like a beacon
Toward new lands and high adventure.

. . . He encountered much more traffic
Than he had anticipated.
There were horsemen, buggies, coaches,
Traveling in both directions.
Huge freight wagons, heavy laden,
Drawn by tandem yokes of oxen,
Rumbled toward the vast plantations.

Hours from Natchitoches he halted
At a spring to fill his canteen
And to let his thirsty horses
Drink their fill of cool, clear water.
Resting under a magnolia
Burdened with big bursting blossoms,
Was a smiling, friendly Frenchman
Who approached him, hand extended,
Saying, "I am Louis Choteau,
Traveling west, and I would welcome
Company. The way grows lonely
After many days of travel."

III

Following the introductions
They proceeded down the dusty

Road to Natchitoches and respite
From the tiresome, weary journey.
As they rode along, the Frenchman
Told of his trip to the markets
In St. Louis where he purchased
Merchandise for his emporium.
He was a successful merchant
In Natchitoches where his forebears
Had been enterprising traders
Ever since the town was founded.

"This fair land through which we travel,"
Said Choteau with pride and gusto,
"Was, and is, the choicest morsel
That America can offer
Men from any land. It truly
Is where French and Spanish cultures
Sank their roots and started growing.
In Seventeen-Fourteen, Frenchmen
Paddled up the long Red River,
Built a fort and trading center—
First French outpost in the Southwest—
Four years prior to the founding
Of New Orleans on the Gulf Coast.

"Fourteen miles west of Natchitoches,
In the year Seventeen-Eighteen,
Spaniards hastened to establish
Los Adaes, the official
Capital of Spanish Texas
For more than half a century.

" . . .Thus the country gently cradled
Two great cultures—French and Spanish.

29

Had not greed and lust and envy
Entered in to spoil the picture,
These two people might have blended
Into a majestic, mighty
Empire with a rosy future."
Givens listened in amazement
As Choteau recited history
In loquacious, charming manner
Till they reached the city's outskirts.
At Choteau's polite insistence
Newton tarried there till morning.

Following an early breakfast
Newton and his host departed
For the store to get some items
Newton needed to replenish
The provisions for his journey.

IV

The emporium was crowded
With a group of laughing, joking
Dragoons from the Indian country.
As a clerk approached, announcing:
"This is Captain Cato Rutledge
From Washita, Monsieur Choteau.
He would like some information."
Newton glanced about, half hoping
That his quest had ended early . . .
But the colonel was not present.

"I am seeking a Lieutenant
Randolph Marcy who is due here
With a company of soldiers

Of the Occupation Army,
On their way to Southern Texas,"
Said the debonair young captain.

"Captain Rutledge," Newton ventured,
"My name's Givens. I am traveling
To Fort Washita on business
With a gentleman named Lovelace . . . "
"*Colonel* Lovelace?" interrupted
Rutledge. Givens nodded, eager
For whatever bit of knowledge
Might be learned about the colonel.
"Colonel Lovelace is no longer
At Fort Washita. He left there
Last week on a special mission
To Bent's Fort. Rampageous Indians
Robbed a wagon train and murdered
Several men who traveled with it.
He has gone to learn the details
And to punish the marauders."

Louis Choteau was successful
In securing news of Marcy
For the captain. When the dragoons
Had departed, Choteau noticed
Bitter disappointment written
On the face of Newton Givens.

"Where is Bent's Fort?" queried Newton.

"It is far away," said Choteau,
"On the plains, in land included
In the Louisiana Purchase.
The Trail to Santa Fe runs by it."
"How far is it?" pursued Newton.

"Captain Rutledge just informed me
That the man I seek has gone there."

"Heavens, man! I cannot rightly
Say, but it is several hundred
Miles by river. As the crow flies,
It is nearer. I would judge that
Seven hundred miles is accurate.

"Many years ago my Uncle
Auguste Choteau was a trader
In that storied land of Indians.
Choteau Mound and Choteau's Island
On the Arkansas are famous
Landmarks in that legendary
Land of mystery and adventure.
Uncle Auguste told me many
Gripping tales about the region.
It is treacherous but winsome."

"I must go there *now*," insisted
Newton to the startled Choteau.

"Times have changed since Uncle Auguste
Lived and traded in that country.
All the way from East Cross Timbers
You must travel through a dangerous
Land of vengeful, hostile red men.
Massacres and Indian raiding
Grow more common with each passing
Moment. The *Comancheria*
And the land beyond is peopled
With determined tribes preparing
To repel the dawning movement
Toward their rich ancestral domains.

It is downright suicidal
For a man unlearned in Indian
Ways to try to make the journey."

"Still, I have to go," said Newton.
"You must help me find assistance.
Surely somewhere there's a party
Who can guide me through the region!"

"Not in Natchitoches!" The answer
Was a blow that staggered Newton.
"I shall go alone," he muttered.

Choteau probed the deep recesses
Of his memory and offered
Renewed hope to troubled Givens:
"There is one in Nacogdoches
Who can help you. Randall Duncan
Was some years ago employed
By the Bents. As a frontiersman,
You will find he has no equal."

With the warm hand clasp of kindred
Souls in circumstance and spirit,
Givens and Choteau were parted.

Traveling onward, ever westward,
Givens listened to the mournful,
Plaintive singing of the darkies
Tending cotton in the rolling
Fields that stretched to the horizon.

Primitive and ancient yearnings
Were reflected in the haunting
Spirituals of depth, revealing
Olden, mystic tribal hunger
For the freedom long denied them . . .

Chapter Four

Gaines Crossing

IT WAS DUSKY dark when Givens
Called a loud hello before the
House that stood beside the highway.
From the doorway came a "Welcome,
Stranger! Light and have some supper."
James Gaines, lately of Virginia,
Built the house along the roadway
On the high bank of the river
In Eighteen Twelve. It was destined
For a role in Southwest history
Undisputed in importance.
It was through the famed Gaines Crossing
Of the froward Sabine River
That a legion of historic
Men first entered lusty Texas.

Gaines House was a happy haven—
Hard beside the storied highway
El Camino Real stretching
From the city of St. Louis
To the Alamo in Texas,
Which had started as a dim trail
In the dimmer past — it nestled

In a grove of pine and sweet gum.
Once the trail knew thundering hoofbeats
Of the buffalo and mustang.
It had felt the cushioned treading
Of moccasins worn by Caddoes,
Stealing down an ancient warpath,
Then the marching boots of soldiers
On their way to rout the British
From New Orleans for Jackson.

Gaines House was first stop in Texas
For a secret frontier army
Headed by Magee-Gutierrez
In revolt against the Spaniards.
They engaged in bloody struggle,
Worse than Texas Revolution,
In three battles in South Texas.
Finally the expedition
Saw its cause collapse in ruin—
Practical annihilation . . .

History crosses off another
Army which had used the crossing:
Dr. James Long marched from Natchez
To Stone Fort in Nacogdoches
Where headquarters were established.
He proclaimed the land of Texas
A republic — independent.
In the end, embattled Spaniards
Captured Long's ill-fated army.
With the death of their commander
At the hands of an assassin,
All the hopes of filibusters
In the Southwest terminated . . .

For a time this door to Texas
Stood wide open. Peaceful entry
Was permitted without question.

A young lawyer, William Travis,
Fleeing an unhappy marriage
In the state of Alabama,
Tarried for a while at Gaines House.
From Tennessee a frontiersman-
Politician, Davy Crockett,
Came to cast his lot in Texas.
Still a second Tennessean
Used this rustic port of entry—
He, too, fled a tragic marriage—
Made his home a few miles distant:
At San Augustine, Sam Houston
Was elected to the office
That led on to San Jacinto
And defeat for Santa Anna.

During the travail of Texas
There was one more fateful crossing
At Gaines Ferry. U. S. Troopers
Cantered through to Nacogdoches
Where they took their battle stations
And prevented reinforcement
Of the Mexicans by Indians,
Thus assisting Houston's victory
In the San Jacinto battle.

II

Five miles west of Gaines House, Givens
Overtook a circuit rider

Heading for McMahan's Chapel
Where he was to hold a service
On the morrow which was Sunday.

"Littleton Fowler is the name,"
Said the hardy frontier preacher.
As they rode along they discussed
The amenities of travel.
It developed that the pastor
Had been named as superintendent
Of the Methodists of Texas.
At San Augustine, he aided
In the founding of Wesleyan
Male and Female College slated
For an early opening, waiting
Now arrival of the teachers.
Fowler also had established
Flourishing McMahan's Chapel,
First Protestant church in Texas.
As they neared the little chapel,
Evening shadows settled softly,
And they noticed an encampment
Of soldiers in the pines that towered
High above the tiny temple . . .
Randolph Marcy was an old friend
Of the pioneering parson.
He had learned that Fowler's schedule
Called for preaching at the chapel
Sunday morning and had waited
To attend the worship service.
He was on his way to southern
Texas to join Taylor's forces.

III

Marcy took a sudden fancy
To the Englishman who traveled
With his friend the circuit rider,
And the compliment was mutual:
Newton knew an instant liking
For the striking young lieutenant,
Saw him as a man of valor,
Dedicated to his duties.
Thus began a cherished friendship:
Trails of these two men were destined
To cross and recross in the future.

Sunday, after church was over,
Givens rode along with Marcy
And his men toward Nacogdoches.
As they journeyed, the lieutenant
Talked of Mary and the children,
And the dreams they dreamed together.

Newton shared his confidences:
Told about his far-flung wanderings
And his meeting with Lucinda;
Spoke of how he hoped to marry
Her and spend the years remaining
Making her the "happiest woman
Ever to walk the way of mortals."

At Stone Fort in Nacogdoches
Marcy said farewell to Givens,
Wishing him a pleasant journey
And a most successful mission;
Told him half in jest to marry,

Then to join the U. S. Army
Where his services were needed.
He could serve a cause full worthy
By promoting good relations
In the frontier lands of Texas.

IV

. . . At the sutler's store young Givens
Asked where he might locate Duncan.
"You will find him at the livery
Barn attending to his horses,"
Said the sutler, "It's the building
With the hitch racks, on the corner."

Although Duncan had the bearing
Of a man inured to hardship,
He had once been a schoolmaster.
He had come to Nacogdoches
In Eighteen Twenty-six with Edwards.
He had fought in the Fredonian
War and also was a veteran
Of successful revolution,
Fighting to the gory ending.

Randall Duncan was acquainted
With the ways of western tribesmen,
Having traded with the Indians
Until growing hostile actions
Brought an end to redskin barter
In the land wherein he traded.

After chatting briefly, Newton
Realized that Louis Choteau
Knew whereof he spoke in saying

39

That if any man could take him
To Bent's Fort, that man was Duncan.

"I am trapped in a dilemma,"
Newton told him. "I must journey
To the hinterland where white men,
So I am told, seldom venture.
I have heard you know the country.
I should like for you to guide me
To Bent's Fort. The urgent business
That necessitates my going
Cannot wait. I leave tomorrow."

Slowly Randall Duncan answered:
"It is true . . . I know the country,
But I also know the hazards
Of the long, uncertain journey
Through a land where Indians daily
Grow more bitter and resentful.
To reach Bent's Fort, one must travel
An enormous stretch of upland—
Timbers, mountains, canyons, rivers,
Foothills, mesas—beauty, danger.
Then at last you reach the rolling
Plains, magnificent and spreading
Like an ocean into distance.
Teeming, seething, onward-rushing
Waves of buffalo and other
Wildlife thrive upon the grassy
Billows which roll on forever.
To some men those plains are lonely,
Terrifying and oppressive,
Verging on the brink of madness . . .

Other men of sterner mettle
Find enchantment, exaltation,
In the vast expansive regions.
Some men cower and cringe before them;
Others don the crown of monarchs—
Some men's hemlock, some men's nectar—
Land that flings a chilling challenge
To the men who seek its secrets . . .

"I cannot resist that challenge;
I shall meet you here at daybreak."

V

. . . Taking a northwest direction
Newton and his guide-companion
Soon had passed the final vestige
Of civilization and had
Entered the domain of Indians.
Late one afternoon the travelers
Topped a hill and in the offing
Some few miles below them saw a
Caravan of covered wagons
Turn and wheel into a circle.

"Freighters," Randall said, "preparing
To make camp in the protection
Of the mesa. There is water
And good grass to graze their oxen."

"I was not aware," said Newton,
"That a road ran through this country."

Randall answered: "It's another
Indication of expansion.
To promote frontier advancement,

41

Some five years ago, aggressive
President Lamar insisted
That a military roadway
Be constructed from Red River
To the Bay of Corpus Christi.

"Congress authorized the building
Of the road. In Eighteen Forty
Colonel William Cook led forces
From the Brazos to Red River
Where Fort Johnson was established
And the road construction started.

"Soon the project was abandoned
Due to lack of funds. But later
The road you see was completed
From Preston Bend on Red River
To San Antonio. Dallas,
Bird's Fort and the Anadarko
Village of Jose Maria,
Torreys' trading posts, and Austin,
All are on or near this marker
Of the far frontier of Texas.

"Intermittent warfare rages
All along the frenzied border.
Well, that's not quite true; there's one place
Where the Indians and the white men
Dwell in peace and trade together.
This I learned, to my amazement,
Early last year when I journeyed
From my home in Nacogdoches
On a trapping expedition.

VI

"Westward probably a hundred
Miles from Parker Brothers' fortress,
On a creek named Tehuacana,
Stands Post Number Two of Torreys'
Several Indian trading houses.
It had been in operation
For a year at my arrival.

"President Sam Houston sanctioned
Building of the posts to better
Our relations with the Indians;
In fact, he is an investor
In the business as are other
Leading citizens of Texas.

"From Connecticut the brothers
David, Thomas, and John Torrey
Came to Texas to establish
These extensive trading centers.

"At the Torrey trading houses—
Unlike Bent's Fort where we're going—
Fortresses are not included
In the layout of the centers.

"In an ocean of bluebonnets,
Like a tranquil fishing village
I once knew on Martha's Vineyard
Off the coast of Massachusetts,
Torreys' outposts are composed of
Six or eight substantial structures
Built of logs for living quarters,
Storage rooms for pelts, and trade goods,

And the trading post where Indians
Mingle freely with the traders.

"The relationship existing
Between Torreys and the Indians
Is, indeed, a revelation.
Both sides seem to take great pleasure
In the free flow of their commerce.
They prefer it evidently
To exchange of whistling bullets
And the whine of flying arrows.

"Some four miles from Torrey Brothers'
Number Two Post is the council
Ground where white men meet with Indians
To negotiate their treaties.

VII

"Last October I was privileged
To be present when Sam Houston,
Whom I knew in Nacogdoches,
Counseled with Comanche chieftains
And their allies. Houston told them
That the clean white pathway traveled
By both races at the present
Need not evermore know bloodshed.

" 'President Lamar,' said Houston,
'In his eagerness to settle
Frontier lands has broken treaties
And dealt shamefully with Indians;
But this treatment, I assure you,
Shall not, must not, be repeated.'

"Standing head and shoulders over
Most of the romantic figures
In our storied land of Texas,
Houston, an adopted tribesman
Of the Cherokees, has always
Championed the rights of Indians.

"It is ever his contention
That bad faith expressed by white men,
Treaty-breaking and aggression,
Are responsible for troubles
Now existing between red men
And the government of Texas.

"He says Indians are entitled
To an honorable solution
Of the problems that develop
Through colonial expansion.
Abstract qualities of justice
Show in all of Houston's dealings
With the entire run of redskins.

"He is criticized and censured,
But I somehow have a feeling
He is right . . . that they are human.

"Common attitude of Texans
Toward the Indians is contemptuous,
Vitriolic hatred, seasoned
With an avaricious craving
For the Indians' land and birthright."

As the conversation ended,
They entered the camp of freighters.

"Hi, there!" rang the booming voice of
Arden Temple, who commanded
The wagon train. "Won't you join us?
Buffalo and beans for supper . . .
Visitors are always welcome,
'Less they're hunting scalps or trouble!"

"It will be a pleasure," Newton
Said and swung from off his saddle.

Randall took the mounts and hobbled
Them and turned them out to pasture.
After the delicious supper,
Newton learned from Arden Temple
That the wagon train was taking
Trade goods and supplies to Torreys'
Trading centers, and to Austin.

Soon the tired and weary freighters
Sought the comfort of their bed rolls.

Talking quietly beside the
Dying embers of the camp fire,
Randall talked about his favorite
Subject: Texas and its future.

"I am interested," said Newton
In the Torrey Brothers' trading
Houses — and the Tehuacana
Country I find fascinating . . .
Could you tell me more about them?

VIII

"Yes," said Randall, "I'll be glad to:
"Tehuacana hills surrounding

Tehuacana Creek are laden
With a peaceful rugged beauty.

"Once the area was peopled
By the Tawakoni Indians.
Tawakonis were a powerful
Tribe, quite civilized, moundbuilders.
In the latter Eighteen Twenties
Destiny prescribed near finish
For the clan. Like many other
Tribes, they were almost destroyed.
Strangely, it was not the white man
That wrote finis to their culture;
It was Cherokees, another
Nation driven from its homeland
By land-hungry, scheming white men.

"In the ultimate heroic
Stand upon the highest hilltop,
Thick, dry grass was fired, and raging
Flames engulfed the Tawakonis.
They were virtually destroyed;
But the young son of the chieftain,
Smuggled from the flaming hilltop,
Lived, and legend says the spirit
Of the chieftain waits and watches
For returning of his offspring
To avenge the Tawakonis.
Through the years the legendary
Ghost appears at dawn and twilight,
Slowly scans the hills and valleys,
Disappears, and waits in silence.

"Once when riding near the hilltop
While the evening shadows gathered,
I beheld an ancient Indian
Gazing westward toward the sunset.
He was not a ghost, I'm certain . . .
Still, at my approach he faded
Into nothingness . . . an eerie
Rustling . . . wind, I guess . . . pervaded
All the land and seemed to murmur:
'He will come, mayhap, tomorrow . . .
But I know it does not matter
If he comes at all, for surely
The divided Indian people
Now have traveled down the wrong trail
Past the point of no returning . . .
Tawakoni and the other
Indian tribes are lost forever . . . '

"I do not believe in spirits,
Still there's something downright spooky
In the Tawakoni legend . . .

"I have talked enough for one night,
I will see you in the morning."

"Good," said Newton, "let us slumber."

On the morrow, after breakfast,
Which was served at crack of dawning,
Randall saddled up the horses
While the freighters harnessed oxen.
Quick good-bys were said and freighters
Headed south . . . while to northwestward
Randall rode with Newton Givens . . .

Several hours of uneventful
Travel brought them to the land of
East Cross Timbers. It divided
Hunting grounds of peaceful Indians
Who resided in East Texas
And the Kiowas-Comanches,
And of other tribes residing
On the plains of Western Texas,
Fierce and warring and protective
Of the ranges that supplied them
Buffaloes which formed their larder.

Pushing toward their destination,
Through a virgin land of beauty,
Randall talked in tones of rapture
Of the land he had adopted:

"Texas knows the magic moment
When a glowing, gripping chapter
In the tome of time is ended.
Now we turn the page not knowing
How the tale will be completed.
We have witnessed many wonders:
Sunrise, sunset, mystic midnight,
Dying time and hour of birthing—
When one age becomes another.

"I have watched with keenest interest
The establishment of Texas
As a spunky young republic.
I have seen the strains and stresses
Of its newborn independence
Become greater than financial
Resources can say grace over.

I will welcome annexation
Which is pending now in Congress.

"Growing pains are running rampant
Through the crude untutored giant,
And I say, with annexation,
Texas will become outstanding
In the Sisterhood United."

Forging onward through Cross Timbers
They came to the plains outstretching
To the farther hills and mesas.
Drenched with sunlight, gently pulsing
With the breathing wind, the gorgeous
Landscape was, indeed, inspiring:
Pastel faces of the flowers
Poked above the lush green grasses;
Antelope and deer and mustangs
Added to the panorama
Of serenity and beauty.
In midafternoon the travelers
Saw the markings of the river,
And by twilight they were eating
Supper by the tumbling Brazos.

IX

Camping there beside the waters,
Resting on their outspread bedrolls,
When the fire had burned to embers,
Randall fell to reminiscing:

"There's a story old and hoary
Called the Legend of the Brazos.
I believe you might enjoy it.

"In the distant past when Texas
Was a Spanish Crown possession,
Long before the Pilgrim Fathers
Sailed across the wide Atlantic,
Coronado led a party
Of explorers through the plainsland
Searching for the Seven Cities
With their storied golden treasure.
Many moons they chased the phantom
Of the Cities of Cibola.
But their quest went unrewarded
For the shrewd old Indian chieftain
Who had sent them on the journey
Reasoned that the plains would lead them
To a land of no returning.

"Lost, the expedition suffered
Tortures of the damned; their water
Was exhausted and their fevered
Minds no longer gave direction
To their footsteps; thus they wandered
Aimlessly into a valley.

"Summoning the full remainder
Of his strength, the famished *padre*
Asked the men to kneel for unction,
Sacrament, before they perished.
Sobered by the priestly gesture,
Every babbling tongue was silenced.
As they bowed an awsome stillness
Settled over the broad valley,
And a miracle was witnessed:
Borne on softly soughing zephyr

Came the sound of flowing water—
God had led them to a river!

"When their pangs of thirst were vanquished,
And their senses were returning,
All eyes rested on the *padre*.
Through the stillness yet unbroken,
But for rippling of the water,
Solemn words arose to heaven:
'Saved by *los Brazos de Dios*
(The arms of God) Lord, we thank Thee.'

"There are skeptics who will tell you
That the legend of the naming
Of the Brazos (long since shortened)
Is an old wives' tale, not worthy
Of the credence some men give it.

"But if one day you should wander
To a certain Brazos valley,
And but listen to the singing
Of the onward flowing river,
You can hear the words once uttered
By a grateful Spanish *padre*:
'Saved by *los Brazos de Dios*'—
Arms that never fail the faithful."

"Beautiful," commented Newton,
"Now good night, my bones are weary."

Chapter Five

Clear Fork Country

TWO DAYS LATER they had entered
Lush and verdant Clear Fork country.
In a wide inviting valley
Near a spring of purling water,
Fresh and fragrant as the dewdrops,
Givens said: "Although it's early,
I should like to spend the night here,
Rest, and just admire the splendor
Of this inspiring virgin country."

They pitched camp and Randall started
Staking out the wearied horses.
Under trees that lined a pretty
Creek toward which the cool spring trickled
Was a flock of turkeys scratching
In the mast beneath the oak trees.
Tired of venison and bear meat,
Randall drew his Long Tom rifle;
Then again he gauged the distance,
Pulled his pistol from its scabbard,
Fired one shot and felled a turkey.
Startled by the sharp explosion,
Animals and birds poised, ready

For instant flight if another
Sound disturbed their lazy feeding.
After a few restless moments,
All was quiet again and peaceful.

As Randall made preparations
To roast the turkey for their supper,
Newton gazed in spellbound rapture
At the scene outspread before him.
Near at hand a rounded summit,
Rising like a lofty altar,
Beckoned him and he responded.
Up the crest in growing wonder,
Pausing often to examine
Varied aspects of the picture,
Climbed the captivated rover.

From the height he gulped the nectar
Of the heady panorama . . .
Saw a masterpiece, a painting
From the brush of Master Artist,
Painted with rich molten sunbeams
On the canvas of creation . . .
The Old Testament recording
Of the Eden known by Adam
Could have been no more impressive
Than the paradise that greeted
The enchanted Newton Givens.

In the distance, staggered mesas
Rose and fell in perfect rhythm—
Marching on across the ages—
Turning landscapes into music
Like the sacred psalms of David,

Soothing, restful, awe-inspiring.

In the valley, broad and fertile,
Carpeted with grama grasses,
Wildlife ranged in rife profusion.
Buffaloes and deer and mustangs
Shared with antelope and other
Animals the fruitful acres.
Hillsides rising from the valley
Flamed with flowers of all descriptions.
Birds of many types and colors
Added to the scene primeval.
Distant howlings indicated
Predatory beasts abounded
In the woods along the river
And the rimrocks of the canyons
Far beyond the vale so tranquil,
Which was weaving Newton Givens
In a spell of new endeavor.

II

Never in his distant travels
Had he heard a voice so plainly
Speak to him in the arresting
Eloquence of God's creation.

While his soul drank in the beauty,
He was filled with contemplation
And a yearning for Lucinda . . .
As he watched the shaggy bison
Browsing in the knee-deep grasses,
They were transformed into cattle,
Fat and sleek like those seen grazing

In the undulating pastures
By the Mississippi River . . .
Then his vision was expanded
To the far-flung land a-rolling
On and on to the horizon:
Antelopes became merinos
That would furnish fleece for fabric
Of a quality well suited
For his bride-to-be, Lucinda,
And the children she would bear him . . .

On the mustangs hard below him
There appeared gay, laughing riders
Following the deer and foxes
In the olden sport of Britain . . .

As his dream grew in dimension,
He beheld imposing structures
Rising near the creek that wandered
Lazily into the Clear Fork . . .

The ranch plant that he envisioned
Was impressive . . . It included
A distinguished group of buildings
And corrals of fine construction,
Built to long withstand the bludgeon
Of the elements' untiring
Wear and tear and ceaseless beating.

Furniture would be imported
From the marts of France and England:
Theirs would be the gracious living
Of the Old World — far transplanted
To the borderland of Texas . . .
Aye, their home would be a love song,

A sonata like Beethoven's
That would soar on wings of splendor
To the very dome of heaven,
To the portals of the angels,
Keeping faith with dreams of youthful
Lovers since the world's beginning . . .

Newton Givens, born romancer,
Thus soliloquized, enraptured:
"Here in this expansive recess,
To infinity far-stretching,
Floored from hill to hill with carpets
Of rich grass and richer flowers,
With animals and birds abounding,
Home has waited through the ages
For my coming. I preempt it.
This fair land has won forever
My approval and allegiance.
Here, somehow, I'll bring Lucinda:
Here we'll spend our lives together . . .
Paradise on earth, inviolate."

Time stood still and then turned backward,
Givens heard the gentle murmur
Of a still small voice so solemn
That it seemed to come from eons
When the earth was in the making,
When the virgin Clear Fork Valley
Knew no man, not even Indians.
When it only knew the splendor
Of its own primeval beauty
And the spirit of its Maker.

III

Here the golden thread was broken
By a dust cloud far to northward
In the dim and hazy distance.
As he watched the far-off duster,
Forms took shape and he distinguished
What he thought might be an army
On the move and coming toward him.

. . . Lying near the smouldering campfire,
Slowly turning roasting turkey,
Randall noticed an uneasy
Movement of the mustangs grazing
Just beyond the silver brooklet.

Quickly he swung into action:
Placed his ear upon the surface
Of the earth and heard a rumbling,
Sound of many hooves approaching.
He doused the fire; grabbed the turkey,
Wrapped it in a piece of doeskin
And ascended to the summit
For a look about the country.

Givens sat beside a boulder
Wondering what the strange procession
Meant when Randall came abreast him,
Saw the sight, knew in an instant
What was happening and beckoned
Givens into the seclusion
Of a natural point of vantage
In a crevice where in safety
They could reconnoiter, figure

Some way out of the position
Into which they'd blindly stumbled.

As the cavalcade drew nearer,
They could see the men and women
And the gay excited children
With their happy, carefree faces
Beaming in anticipation
Of the great hunt in the offing
For the fat wild game that foraged
In great herds throughout the region.

At the campsite, squaws, assisted
By the older children, hastened
To unload the *travois* bulging
With supplies—food, teepees, bedding,
And the other necessary
Items to provide the frugal
Comforts of the hardy tribesmen.

All routine domestic duties
Were performed by squaws, slaves, children.
Braves confined their manly interests
To the skills of their forefathers—
Hunting buffaloes . . . and warfare.

Setting up the clustered teepees
Was a task of short duration.
Four long tent poles, cedar saplings,
Were expertly lashed together
At the tops and then spread outward
From the bottom, forming frameworks
Which were covered with close-fitted
Buffalo hides, giving shelter

From the blazing heat of summer
And the icy blasts of winter.

Skins were hung with flesh side outward,
Lending tints of white and yellow
To the coloring of shelters.
In the center was a fire pit
To provide for warmth and cooking.
Overhead an oval opening
Pulled the smoke up through the vertex.

While the squaws assembled teepees,
Boys and slaves were tending horses,
Fetching water from the river,
Stacking firewood and attending
To the other chores allotted
Them in making preparation
For their stay in Clear Fork Valley.

As the witching hour of twilight
Veiled the land in shades of purple,
Loneliness crept through the vastness;
But the camp was quick to counter
With a cheerfulness and bustle
That bespoke a calm assurance:
All is well and the Great Spirit
Is watching over all His children.

Long the horses had been pastured
In the meadow by the river.
Long the camp had been in order,
And the evening meal was finished.
Every chore had been completed.
Now each member of the household

Found a place of cheery comfort
To enjoy the pleasant session
Of instructive story-telling.

From within the lighted teepees,
Glowing like gigantic lanterns,
Squaws in fringed and beaded buckskin
Listened as the braves in fancy
Breechclouts, moccasins, and leggings
Chanted to the cadenced beating
Of the haunting, muted tom-toms.
Children in respectful silence
Heard again enthralling stories
Told by contemplative chanters:
Tribal culture and traditions,
Ancient rituals and folklore,
Epics of heroic actions
By the olden braves and chieftains
Passed in this entrancing manner
To succeeding generations.

IV

Twilight blended into nighttime
As a deep red moon climbed slowly
From behind a distant mesa.
Flames died lazily in fire pits,
And the smoke was wafted upward
To combine its misty vapors
With the blue haze overspreading
Nestled teepees with a mantle
Of protection from the awesome
Blood upon the moon foretelling

61

Tragic times for the Comanches
And the debonair young lover—
Handsome, gallant Newton Givens.

"What a peaceful scene," said Newton,
We have witnessed here this evening
With the coming of the tribesmen.
Tell me why so much unhappy
Feeling flows between the races
Of the white men and the red men."

V

"Through the centuries *The People*,"
Randall told him in responding,
"Known to others as Comanches,
Have reigned as roving, undisputed
Lords of vast and verdant rangelands
From the Arkansas extending
To the Lower Rio Grande.
Both the Spaniard and Apache
Have supremacy conceded
To these bands of stalwart nomads,
Bent on following the shaggy
Buffaloes which are their mainstay.
Aye, Comanches' economic
Lifeblood flows from buffalo herds—
They provide a common market:
Steak and pemican and *charqui*
Form the basis of their diet.
Too, they find the blood refreshing
As a drink and appetizer.

"Hides, in turn, are sheaths for teepees,
Travois coverings, and war shields.
Better hides are tanned, made into
Articles of fine apparel:
Leggings, breeches, skirts and jerkins,
Head bands, moccasins, and breechclouts.
Cooking implements are made of
Bones, as are knives, awls, and needles.
Larger of the horns are used in
Their religious ceremonies.
From the tendons, entrails, bladder,
They make many things including
Bowstrings, sacks and water bottles.
Fine long hair from manes, or forelocks,
Furnish other useful items:
Woven belts and strong *reatas;*
Also ornaments and knickknacks,
Dolls and playthings for the children.
And the chips are used for fuel
As the area is treeless,
Save along the creeks and rivers.
Buffaloes are interwoven
In their culture and traditions.
Some of their most sacred dances
Are devoted to the stately
Animals from which they garner
Most of their humble requirements.

"In the heyday of their tenure
They were happy and contented,
Living well from off the bounty
Granted them by the Great Spirit.

Now with white men pushing closer
To their cherished hunting ranges,
They grow restless, stubborn, warlike . . .
Blood will surely flow in torrents
If we do not find solutions
To the problems that are mounting
Rapidly between the cultures
Of the paleface and the redskin . . .

"We must leave here before morning.
If alert scouts should discover
Us, we probably would suffer
Death at their hands for intruding
On the lands they call their birthright."

. . . Givens nibbled cold roast turkey
As he helped to get the horses
Ready for a fast departure.
Looping far southward, they traveled
All that night. In early morning,
As the sun was kindling blazes
On the faraway horizon,
They encamped in wooded cover
Many miles beyond the Clear Fork.

Chapter Six

Canyonland and Plains

. . . TRAVELING AT a lively canter,
Randall said, "The country changes,
Gradually it grows more rugged."

Soon they entered a majestic
Canyonland of charm and splendor
Filled with palaces, cathedrals,
Citadels and countless other
Lovely, strange, fantastic structures.
Beautifully eroded castles
Towered toward the turquoise heavens.
Churches chisled from the limestone
By the hands of master sculptors:
Wild wind, hard rain, pounding sandstorm,
Working patiently through ages
Without end to gain perfection,
Swiftly won absorbed approval
Of the first white men to see them.

"Mortals strayed into a garden
Made for gods . . . We are trespassers,"
Newton said in admiration,
"This sight beggars all description."

. . . Lying near the dying embers
Of the evening fire relaxing,
Following a long day's journey,
Newton voiced appreciation
For the courtesies which Randall
Showered upon him as they traveled:

"I appreciate the earthy
Knowledge which you have imparted.
You have made this scenic, fruitful
Country come alive. The hazards
Of the trip are obviated
Through the majesty and wonder
Of your magical disclosures.

"In addition to the sightly
Herds of buffaloes, wild horses,
You have shown me forms of wildlife
That I never knew existed:
Horned toads, prairie dogs, and chipmunks;
Woodchucks, porcupines, o'possums;
Coyotes, raccoons, *javelinas;*
Snowy bighorns keeping sentinel
From the lofty crags above us.
Tawny killers of the rimrocks:
Bobcats, panthers, mountain lions.

"You have shown me fowls of many
Kinds: wild turkeys, prairie chickens,
Pheasants, quails — a hundred other
Birds that one can scarce imagine
Run the scale of size and color—
Humming birds to mighty eagles.
Hordes of insects you have pointed

Out to me, explaining clearly
All you know about their habits.
Things that walk, creep, fly, and slither
Seem as commonplace and natural
As if I had always known them.
You have been a well-versed mentor,
Thank you . . . See you in the morning."

II

Next day, shortly before noontide,
Well advanced in Great Plains country,
Bands of antelope grew frequent.
Showing usual fascination
For all creatures, Newton stated:
"I believe they are more graceful
Than any animal encountered
On our journey up to this time.
I would like to get a closer
View, but they all keep their distance."

"If you will dismount. I'll show you
How we may attract them to us,"
Randall said and stopped the horses.

Lying on the ground, well hidden
By the grass in which they waited,
Randall placed a colored kerchief
On his ramrod, gently waved it
Till the pronghorns — graceful phantoms
Of the plainsland — circled nearer:

Marching, halting with precision
That would shame a well-drilled soldier.
Soon they were quite close, and Newton
Marveled at their nimble movements.

Randall aimed his Long Tom rifle,
Cocked it, slowly squeezed the trigger.
At the first shot, off they scampered
Till in graceful bounds they faded
Like clouds scudding into distance.
One remained to make a tasty
Dinner for the hungry travelers.

III

Pushing forward toward the sunset,
Newton said: "Your apt description
Of the plains, before we started,
Was intriguing and I wondered
How they would affect my being . . .

"Plains remind me of the oceans:
The magnificence of distant
Horizons rapidly receding
Into loneliness and vagueness
Is found only on the waters
And in this bewitching region.
In the emptiness of nighttime,
Roar and bellowing of bison
Change into the ceaseless beating
Of an ocean on a coastline!
Air is crisp, exhilarating,

Like the air that sails the oceans!
Resembling seas, plains are subject
To capricious whims of nature:
Violent gales and savage cloudbursts,
Vicious, raging, wild tornadoes—
Sounds that deafen, sharp contrasting
The solemnity and awesome
Stillness of the dead calm, silence!

"These tumultuous grassy billows,
Rolling, swelling into endless
Waves that sweep forever onward,
Look for all the world like water,
Surely, they are close related!

"Here and there the sea is broken
By an island sharply rising
From the depths: a lonely landmark
Left by time to trace its passing.
Buttes are ancient ships abandoned
By the gods in olden ages
When their quest for Eden ended."

IV

. . . Nearing Horse Creek, Randall motioned
With his right hand toward a lengthy
Train of wagons slowly snaking
Toward them. Newton asked in wonder:
"Where on earth did they all come from?"

"Westport," Randall grinned, "Missouri.
We have reached the rolling, twisting
Trail to Santa Fe — behold it!"

69

Bull whips popped and loud resounding
Wo-ha's rang across the prairie.
Drovers dressed in quaint, tight-fitting
Pantaloons, fur caps, checked wool shirts
Challenged Newton's quick appraisal.
Chatting with the wagon master,
Invitation was extended
Them to join the prairie schooners
For the little time remaining
Till they reached the fabled fortress . . .

Chapter Seven

Hinterland Fortress

LIKE A CITADEL of ancient
Ages rising from the bosom
Of the wide, expansive plainsland,
Bent's Fort was a fair oasis
In a land of never-never.

William Bent, a prince of traders,
Built the fort and made his home there.
Bent and St. Vrain were rivals
Of the Astors for the riches
Flowing from the western fur trade.

As the caravan crept nearer,
Travelers found that they were facing
An extensive wall with loopholes
Peeking through the topmost section.
At the left end towered a bastion,
Showing portholes for the cannon.
At the right end, equidistant,
Rose a sightly second story.

Over iron-bound gate a blockhouse
Looked out far across the country.

Perched upon the gate-house was a
Slatted wooden belfry caging
One brass bell and two live eagles.
From atop the lofty belfry,
Floating in the constant breezes,
Waved Old Glory, soft proclaiming:
"All is well within my shadow."

From the left end of the rear wall
Rose a second bastion, housing
Powder, cannon, ammunition;
Walls were hung with guns and lances
Evidencing preparation
To resist whatever forces
Might be hurled against the stronghold.

Near the gate a cemetery
Sheltered the remains of members
Of the family who had perished.

Newton watched with avid interest
The events as they unfolded
Deep in wildest Indian country.
By the time the weary drivers
Had corralled exhausted charges,
The parapet was lined with many
People set to greet the strangers.

The establishment employed
Traders, teamsters, packers, hunters,
Blacksmiths, hostlers, clerks and servants;
With their families, the number
Pointed upward toward a hundred.

Slowly double gates swung open
To admit the jaded travelers.
Through a deep and shady tunnel
They walked into a *placita*
Which was smoothly paved with gravel.
In the center was a robe press
Where the hides were neatly folded,
Flattened, bound for proper shipment.
On the far side was a well sweep
Slanted toward the dome of heaven.

Wide around the huge *placita*
Roofs of single-storied quarters,
Sloping inward and projecting,
Formed a portico supported
By great wooden, weathered pillars.
From the rear a blacksmith's hammer
Beat a jolly anvil chorus
As the smithy fashioned horseshoes
For a handsome jet-black stallion.
Down the ladder from the roof tops
Poured the residents to welcome
Pilgrims and provide the comforts
Of the celebrated fortress.

Robert Bent, William's brother,
Recognizing Randall, beckoned
Him and Newton up a stairway
To the lavish second-story
Quarters of the old Fort's master.
After introductions, Andrew,
Darky bar-keep, served mint juleps.

Newton learned upon inquiry
That the colonel and the troopers
Were expected any moment
To return to their headquarters
Just beyond the fort's enclosure.
It was understood their mission
Was successful. Final details
Were in process of conclusion.

Following a hearty repast,
Newton and his guide accompanied
Gracious William Bent upon a
Personally conducted survey
Of the trading post and fortress.

Ground floor was composed of many
Spacious rooms with low-beamed ceilings.
Whitewashed walls of smooth adobe,
Earthen floors, now freshly sprinkled
With the cooling crystal water
From the deep well in the courtyard,
Left a clean smell in their nostrils.

In a warehouse, William pointed
Out the merchandise he traded
To the Indians for their peltries.
It included belts and buckles,
Hawk bells, finger rings, steel bracelets;
Hatchets, knives, and an assortment
Of utensils used for cooking:
Big brass kettles, tin pans, boilers;
Bone beads, combs, and looking glasses;
Bear traps, smaller traps for muskrats,

Otters, beavers, and the other
Animals they trapped for barter;
Lead and powder horns, steel lances,
And all sorts of fancy trinkets
Treasured by the several Indian
Tribes with whom the partners carried
On their trading operations.
Stored with these were bags of coffee,
Sugar, hard-tack, raisins, crackers;
Salt pork, red beans, syrup, spices,
Peppersauce and saleratus.

Burdened shelves were stacked with dry goods:
Bolts of calico and cambric;
Gay-hued blue and scarlet strouding;
Shirting, shawls, domestic cotton;
Crepe and bombazine and velvet;
Blood-red threepoint Nor'west blankets.
"Indians like the brighter colors,"
Bent explained to beaming Givens.
Passing on to other sections,
William pointed out the lance-heads,
Trace guns, ox shoes, parts for wagons.
"This we call 'the cellar'," William
Mused and nodded at the big kegs
Of brandy, rum and Taos Lightning.

"Never sell the stuff to 'heathens,'
Keep it for my 'Christian' brothers."

Passing through a roomy parlor
With highly polished central pillars,
Newton noted stacks of blankets,
Mattresses and bales of shaggy

Buffalo robes, used for seating,
Placed around the walls. A table
Held a wooden pail of water
With two rustic golden dippers
Made of gourds which grew profusely
In an irrigated garden.
In addition to the quarters
Occupied by blacksmith, barber,
Carpenter, and jack-of-all-trades,
There were twenty-two bedchambers
In the fort for help and transients.

Upstairs, near the sumptuous chambers
Of the Bents, were office spaces
For the chief clerks, foremen, hunters.
Here, too, was a game room boasting
One and only billiard table
West of the Missouri River.

II

In the evening a fandango
Was arranged for guests. The callers
Whooped it up in frontier fashion.
Fiddlers played the gay, light-hearted
Tunes that chased away the troubles
Of the trail and changed the clumsy
Shoes of dancers into graceful
Magic Cinderella slippers.
For the moment they were masters
Of a universe of pleasure.
Newton's thoughts flashed fondly backward

To a ballroom in the Crescent
City where he held Lucinda
While they floated to the music
Of a waltz from far Vienna.

III

Loneliness was etched on Newton's
Countenance when Robert asked him
If he would enjoy a walk through
The inviting, cool *placita*.
Intrigued by the sincere interest
Newton evidenced in Indians,
Robert told him of the founding
Of the fort in redskin country.

"At the start we four Bent brothers,
George and Charles, William, and I
Joined with St. Vrain in trading
With the Sioux in northern country.
When the Cheyenne tribe divided
Into north and south divisions,
We accompanied the southern
Branch into a virgin country
Theretofore unknown by white men.

"Fountain Creek, our destination,
Was a fairyland of wonders.
The Great Spirit had provided
Everything the tribesmen needed
For a life of ease and plenty.

"Yellow Wolf, the Cheyenne chieftain,
Gave us Indian names, and William

Married the enchanting daughter
Of the Keeper of the Arrows—
The Cheyennes became his brothers.

"Many people said the marriage
Was a mockery. That William
Married only for convenience—
An assist to exploitation
Of the Cheyennes and the other
Tribes with whom we do our trading—
What a lie! They love each other
And are most ideally mated.
He who would disparage squaw men
Is a charlatan and bigot!

"After many moons of living
In that land of happy hunting,
Herds of buffalo diminished;
Once again we journeyed southward.
In Eighteen Twenty-eight, the present
Site of Bent's Fort was selected.

"Passing years have been rewarded
With a fur trade far surpassing
Wildest dreams of all the partners.
In addition to the Cheyennes
We have traded with Apaches,
The Arapahoes, Atsenas,
Kiowas and the Comanches—
Most ferocious of all Indians
Some men call them. Our relations
Have been profitable and wholesome.
We have trusted and respected

Them and we have never witnessed
Indication of deception,
Double-dealing, or dishonor.
This I cannot say of white men
With whom we transact our business.

" . . . If my words sound harsh and caustic,
Please forgive me. My resentment
Of injustice to the Indians
By the average run of white men
Makes me cynical and bitter.

"It is late, my friend, the dancers
Have retired. Should we not join them?"

"You are right," responded Newton.
"Let me thank you for the frankness
Of your story. I am grateful.
Pleasant dreams! Again I thank you
For a most enlightening evening."

IV

An inspiring erubescent
Dawn was flinging flaming firebrands
Through the lower eastern heavens
When Newton, gazing from his window,
Saw the hobbled horses grazing
Out beyond the strong-walled fortress.
Sometime in the night the colonel
Had returned, his mission ended.

. . . Colonel Lovelace, sipping coffee
With his guide-friend, Lone Coyote,
Glanced up as two men approached him.

Disbelief and apprehension
Shook him for a fleeting second:
"It cannot be! Newton Givens!
Shades of Homer! Am I dreaming?
No, you're real. Shake hands, young fellow,
Introduce your friend and tell me
What has happened . . . Mrs. Lovelace?

"No, sir, all is well. Your dear ones
Sent their love and fond affection.
This is Randall Duncan, finest
Guide-companion in the country.
He has taught me natural history
All the way from Nacogdoches."

"Nacogdoches!" boomed the colonel.
"Do you mean you came cross-country,
Rather than the trail? I scarcely
Can conceive of two men traveling
Safely through that land infested
With so many hostile Indians.
Still the story is no stranger
Than the Odessey related
In the quiet of my garden
When we met in Crescent City.
Tell me, what is it that prompted
You to make this perilous journey?"

Newton stammered, "Well, Lucinda
Said that I must ask you . . . That is,
I'm in love with your Lucinda
And have asked her hand in marriage.
She agreed — with your approval."

"This requires some thought," said Lovelace.

"I'll be durned!" exploded Randall.
"I, misogynist and bachelor,
Have been hoodwinked into playing
Nursemaid to a scheming Cupid!"
Newton looked as if a dagger
Had been plunged into his bosom.
"I retract that statement," Randall
Grinned and stretched his hand to Newton.
"I have never known a finer
Man than you are, Givens. Surely
Love that prompts the daring action
You have taken is deserving
Of its ultimate fulfillment.
In sincerity I tell you
It is my fond hope that Colonel
Lovelace gives you his full blessing.
Heartiest congratulations
As of when, and if, he does so."

V

When the morning meal was finished,
Colonel Lovelace issued orders
To make ready for the journey
Back to Washita. Provisions
Purchased at the post were loaded.
Farewells were succinctly exchanged.
Horsemen, ambulance and wagons
Were assembled. The formation
Came to life and headed eastward.

As they rode along the colonel

Told the harsh tale of his mission.
He was worried. Growing tension
On the frontier threatened daily
To erupt in violent bloodshed.

"Can you tell me," Newton questioned,
"How this deadly situation
Came to be? Is there no middle
Ground where sane, unbiased people
Representing both the races
Might work out a sound solution
To their problems, thus avoiding
Heartache, injury, and suffering
Common to this type of conflict?"

Colonel Lovelace gravely answered:
"Deep involvement of two cultures
In diametric opposition
Seems to negate such conclusion.
'Civilized' and 'savage' thinking
Will not brook conciliation.
Right and wrong and moral aspects
Have no bearing on the question—
They are words that only add to
Mad confusion of the subject.

"You, a stranger in our country,
Should hear both sides of the question
Before forming an opinion.

"Story-telling with the Indians
Is a skill quite well developed.
Lone Coyote is a master

Of the art. His erudition
Will amaze you. He is, no doubt,
The most brilliant of Comanches.
Certainly he has prolific
Knowledge of the Indian people.
If you want a comprehensive
Indian viewpoint, let Coyote
Tell you of the red man's problems."

Chapter Eight

Indian Prophet

    . . . LONE COYOTE bore slight furrows
Of advancing age so nobly
That his countenance was given
The expression worn by sages.
His expansive brow receded
In a dignity becoming
Elder statesmen of all races.

Wise in ways of scheming mankind,
He had given up the battle
Of resistance. He was serving
As interpreter for Lovelace.
Reverence for the man filled Givens
As he listened to the tragic
Story told by Lone Coyote . . .

"When a boy of tender summers
Comancheros found me wounded,
Following a gory battle
During which my fellow tribesmen
Had been slain by the Apaches.

"By the time of my recovery,
I had formed a strong attachment

For the *Comanchero* leader,
Juan Montoya, roving merchant,
Who was once a *cibolero*.

"In my travels with the traders,
I became a skillful linguist.
In a few short years I mastered
Some of the Uto-Aztekan,
And a number of Tanoan
Dialects, as well as Spanish,
And a good command of English.

"One spring day our heavy-laden
Caravan of army wagons,
Burros and *carretas* burdened
With a cargo of destruction—
Ammunition, guns and whiskey—
Rendezvoused with the Comanches.

"Blood-stained booty from the ranches,
Wagon trains and *haciendas*:
Women, children, horses, cattle,
Changed hands in the trading session.
When the bartering had ended,
We began the homeward journey
With our fat, enormous profits.

"While encamped at Horsehead Crossing
We were ambushed by a drunken
Party of young bucks who boldly
Told Montoya they had come to
Reclaim all the *contrabando*
Traded to him by their elders.

"Juan Montoya leaped for cover

Underneath an army wagon.
'Kill the crazy fools,' he shouted,
As an arrow pierced his midriff.

"The abortive foray ended,
Raiders scalped the *Comancheros*.
When they came to me, the leader
Said, 'This man is a Comanche;
Do not touch him. He is sorely
Wounded and no doubt will perish.'

"Sometime after the departure
Of the raiders with the plunder,
I could hear the labored screeching
Of a wooden-wheeled *carreta*
As it neared the river crossing.

"Gentle hands of a *Franciscan*
Padre cleansed my wounds and placed me
In the cart and started westward.
In Santa Fe the gracious *padre*
Took me to a monastery
Where he and his good companions
Undertook the long and tedious
Chore of patching up my body.

II

"During months of patient nursing,
I was taught to read and cipher.
Padre Jose, an historian,
Fired in me a zest for learning
All there was to know of Indians.

"The *Franciscan,* celebrated
For his eloquence and wisdom,
Held me spellbound as he taught me
History of Indian nations.
His lucidity of thought and
Clarity of fine expression
Helped me glean the bits of knowledge
Which, when fitted all together,
Coupled with our tribal legends,
Tell the story of my people
And their life within this country.

III

" . . . In the faraway beginning,
Over barren Bering ice floes,
From the land of far Eurasia,
Marched a band of hardy Mongols,
Of Akkadian extraction,
Seeking to relieve the gnawing
Urge of man to find contentment
In a land where all the comforts
Of the fuller life abounded.

" . . . Indians were content and happy
With a minimum of worldly
Goods. Their wealth was in possessing
Songs to sing, expressive dances,
Games and sports for family pleasure,
Evening visits with their neighbors,
Pipes to smoke and thrilling stories
Of heroic deeds accomplished
By the tribesmen and the chieftains.

"They loved to hunt, fish; they gloried
In the gifted imitation
Of the songs of birds; the calling
Of the animals and creatures
Living in the fields and forests.
They liked to glide, swift and noiseless,
Through the valleys, woods, and mountains.

"In the chase and on the warpath,
They showed marvelous endurance.
In the field of agriculture,
Vegetables and plants for weaving
Cloth for garments were developed.
Well-built irrigation systems
Carried water to the patches
Of tobacco, maize, and melons.

"Great inventive skills were practiced
In their stonework, in their weaving.
They excelled in manufacture
Of utensils, wampum, snowshoes,
Pottery, canoes, and items
That upgraded living standards.

"Government, religion, culture
Varied widely with the red men.
Some developed tribal customs
To a high degree, while others
Never left the savage level.

"Primitive? Indeed. But surely
They resembled other races
In their basic moral fibre.
They believed the same Great Spirit
Was the Father of all races.

Those who boast superior culture
Are no different from the Indian
When their homes and lives are threatened.

"Moon on golden moon ascended
As the red men roamed and reveled
Through a world of boundless freedom.

IV

"Europeans brought an end to
Happy hunting grounds of Indians.

"Fifteen Twenty-eight, the fateful
Year the long procession started
With Narvaez and de Vaca,
Initiated endless changes
In the lives of blissful red men.

"Ponce de Leon. De Soto,
Also bent on cruel conquest,
Seeded discontent and distrust
In the hearts of many Indians;
But, of course, in the beginning
There was little indication
Of the maelstrom that was brewing.

"None foresaw that tiny murmurs
Of unrest which Coronado
Left behind him in his questing
For the Cities of Cibola
Would become a raging fury
That must culminate in horror—
A crescendo of destruction—
Which will be resolved when Indians
Are destroyed or subjugated.

"Further seeds of greed and hatred
Sown by Spaniards grew and ripened
Into an unholy harvest.
. . . In this epic's base beginning,
Fifteen Ninety-eight the year was,
Several hundred Spanish settlers
Under Don Juan de Onate
Trudged across the blazing desert
Toward the rumbling Rio Grande.

"On the thirtieth of April
In a sheltering grove of dusty
Cottonwoods they took possession
Of the land . . . of whatsoever
Nature . . . founded in the kingdom . . .
And of all its native Indians . . .

"In that desert-curtained country
Far beyond the help of others,
For three-quarters of a century
Indians suffered cruel enslavement
In the name of 'Christianizing.'

"Through the decades patriotic
Fervor smouldered in the bosoms
Of the Indians. Their ancestral
Way of life was not forgotten.

"Suddenly, in Sixteen Eighty,
There appeared an Indian leader
Who delivered the Pueblos
From the galling yoke of bondage.

"Pope led the fierce rebellion
Which so terrified the Spaniards

They abandoned their possessions,
Fled to Mexico in horror
Of the wrath of freedom rising
From the enmity and fury
Harbored in the hearts of red men.
Pope's stunning stroke of genius
Stands alone in Indian history.
. . . Victory was complete. Pueblos
Regained for a precious moment
Freedom as their forebears knew it.

"In a short time after Spaniards
Fled the wrath of the Pueblos,
Vast herds of abandoned horses
Found their way into the waiting
Hands of eager Southwest Indians.
This new form of transportation
Revolutionized the living
Patterns of the Great Plains dwellers.
They became the most proficient
Horsemen ever known to mankind.

"Rich in game and land and horses,
Indians launched upon the golden
Age that oft precedes the decline
And the fall of mighty people.

"Ownership of land as white men
Understand the phrase was foreign
To the ken of naive red men.
We believed the earth, created
By the hand of the Great Spirit,
Was the property of all men—

Something to be shared in common.
'Selling' land to us meant granting
Paleskins rights to occupy it
Just as we did. We would never
'Sell,' as whites define the meaning
Of the word, our precious birthright.

"The brutal and iconoclastic
Hands of progress and advancement—
Civilization, paleskins call it—
Threaten with obliteration
Every vestige of the culture
Sacred to downtrodden redskins.

"Broken promises and treaties,
Cold deceit and black betrayal
Mark the path the red man travels
Toward that certain end of glory
Known before the white man's coming.

"Tentacles of fate grow tighter;
Destiny in bold handwriting
Pencils 'finis' on the crumbling
Wall of Indians' fond traditions—
We shall know no more forever
Happy trails where walked our fathers."

V

"Lone Coyote," Newton parried,
"Your prophetic story haunts me.
. . . Still, en route to Bent's Fort country
I was witness to Comanches
Moving southward in majestic

Splendor. They seemed joyful, carefree.
Can the future be so ugly,
Grim, repulsive as you paint it?
Do you not believe there still is
Hope for reconciliation?"

Lone Coyote's answer sounded
Like a death knell, cold, relentless:

"You were fortunate in viewing
What may be the last migration
Of importance for Comanches.
History is now repeating
Chapter after sordid chapter
Written on the land that stretches
From the shores of the Atlantic
Past the muddy Mississippi.
Life in its resplendent glory
Dwindles rapidly for red men.
Even now the paleface pushes
Toward the rolling plains of Texas.
Soon the towering Rocky Mountain
Regions will be claimed and taken.
Land that borders the Pacific
Long has been a prized possession
Of the Spaniards. Doom is certain.
We are crushed between two evils.
Ways of life known by our fathers
Disappear into the limbo
Of oblivion . . . forgotten!
Lo! the brimming, bursting largess
Given us by our Great Spirit

Fades away. Stark famine beckons
Down a trail of destitution,
Hunger, grief, extermination.
There is no escape from white men's
Greed for land. The bow and arrow
Fall before more powerful weapons.

"Nevermore, alas, forever!
Shall the buffaloes and Indians
Rove the length and breadth of endless
Prairie lands in boundless freedom . . .
All too few are moons remaining
Until perfidy and fleecing
Mark the end of Indian domains.

" . . . Had the red men only listened
To Tecumseh . . . But they would not!
You have heard me. I have spoken."

Pathos, heartbreak, and compassion
Marked the sad patrician features
Of the prophet, Lone Coyote.

Chapter Nine

The Colonel's Consent

COLONEL LOVELACE beckoned Newton
Toward the ambulance, suggesting:
"While the trail is smooth and level,
We can ride along in comfort
In the ambulance. A julep
Will refresh us. We can visit.
William Bent, forethoughted Yankee,
Packed some mint and ice in sawdust,
Said there might be an occasion
When a cool one would come handy.
This could well be that occasion.

"You, mayhap, surmised the reason
I invited you to join me
Here where we can talk at leisure.
As a son-in-law, you please me;
I admire your forthright manner.
In the diadem of virtues
There is not a star more lustrous
Than sincerity . . . and you have
Been sincere in full disclosure
Of your past. Your reckless living
Cannot be condoned. The spirit

Of atonement manifested
Is commendable. The evil
One does, whether real or fancied,
Is forgiven in the striving
For the higher goal — perfection,
Which, of course, is never mastered.

"My concern is for Lucinda.
I respect her wishes; surely,
I believe in her good judgment—
But your lives have been so different.
We have sheltered and protected
Her from all the seamy features
Life presents . . . Its tribulations
Will come soon enough. The countless
Disappointments flesh is heir to
Come to all. Fate shows no favor.

"Looking backward, I remember
When I wore the shoes you now wear;
When the tender reassuring
Strength that is associated
With the first ecstatic bursting
Of young love consumes the being . . .

"Love and marriage and contingent
Benefits are the most precious
Gifts that God can give to mankind—
Like religion, they are sacred;
They are things to cherish always,
Treasured joys that last a lifetime:
Founding of a home, arrivals
Of the children; the achievements,
Large and small, that etch the pattern

Of expanding love and fuller
Happiness that thrives on problems
Common to the lot of mortals.

"I must stop philosophizing
And get down to the conditions
On which I can give my blessing
To your marriage to Lucinda.
It is a foregone conclusion
That you must exchange allegiance
To America from Britain.
Citizenship can be granted,
After due examination,
By Fort Washita officials.
Next, a gainful occupation
Comes up for consideration.
Your financial independence
Does not preclude obligation
To assist with plans of progress
And expansion for our nation.

"Randolph Marcy, whom you mentioned
Meeting at McMahan's Chapel,
Seems to be a dedicated
Soldier of the type most needed
By our country in the struggle
To develop full resources
And extend its boundaries westward.

"It is hard to maintain proper
Personnel for installations
On the frontier which is growing
Rapidly as population
In the eastern states increases.

"Your experience and background
Qualify you well for service—
I believe that you would like it.
If you should decide to enlist
In the army, it would please me.
Citizenship could be granted
At the time of your acceptance."
Quick to catch the disappointment
That was traced on Newton's features,
Colonel Lovelace added softly:
"I can help you with both matters;
May, perhaps, be instrumental
In securing a commission
For you from the branch of service
You select. Of course, I'm partial
To the dragoons. I have enjoyed
All the years I have been with them."

"I had hoped, you understand, sir,
You would grant us your permission
Unrestricted and untrammeled.
Still, I understand the wisdom
Backing up the terms upon which
You will sanction our engagement.
I accept them. I am ready
To comply . . . and your assistance
Will be gratefully accepted.

II

"But, in fairness, I must tell you
This seems but a temporary
Measure — serving for the present.
When I have become established

In this land and have my bearings,
I propose to be a rancher . . .
"Near a river down in Texas,
Called the Clear Fork of the Brazos,
I discovered an enchanted
Valley rich in all resources
Necessary to the founding
Of the home I always wanted . . .
One day I shall take Lucinda
To that land of virgin beauty
Where I know we shall be happy.

"It is now in Indian country;
But in sifting through the knowledge
I have gathered since arrival
In this country of swift changes,
It is probable that shortly
I can claim it. I am willing
To await that time, and meanwhile
I will follow your suggestions."

. . . At Fort Washita, the colonel
Read his mail and turned the letters
From Lucinda, sent in his care,
Over to impatient Newton.

The indoctrination given
Givens — military, civic —
Stood him in good stead in passing
Both of his examinations
With exemplary comportment
Toward the creed and course of country.
Through influence of the colonel
Givens started off his army
Service with a two months furlough.

Chapter Ten

Red River Country

JUNE WAS WAXING old when Newton
Said farewell to Colonel Lovelace:
"Sir, I wish that you would join me
On the journey to New Orleans."

"I would like to," said the colonel,
"But I have to go to Texas.
If by some stroke of good fortune,
I complete my mission quickly,
I shall try to take a furlough
And be present at the wedding.

"There's a new port, Karishaven,
Near the place where I am going.
Mayhap, I can get a boat there
And go on to Crescent City.
I have written Mrs. Lovelace
Of my plans. I also cautioned
Her not to depend upon them."

As they traveled toward Fort Towson,
Randall mused: "You make a handsome

Soldier. Uniforms become you.
That one, I must say, is different
From the rags I wore while fighting
In the Texas Revolution."

II

Dragoon uniforms, indeed, were
Colorful and quite impressive.
Trousers were pale blue in color,
With a sash that blended neatly,
Topped by dark blue fitted jacket
Trimmed with braid of glowing orange.
Shoulders were adorned with brass scales
Designed to turn strokes of sabers
In a hand-to-hand engagement.
Toughened-leather, highly polished
Gauntlets added to protection
For the hands and wrists and forearms.

Black hat bore a looped eagle
At the right side, and the left side
Trailed with bright plumes of the ostrich.

The uniform was completed
With a flowing cape, or talma,
With loose sleeves permitting action
Of the arms without obstruction.
It extended to the boot tops.

Arms consisted of a Perry
Carbine, Navy Colt revolver,
And a dragoon saber carried

By a saber belt. The cartridge
Box was made of gutta-percha.

III

When the riders reached Fort Towson,
They could sense a keen excitement
As a caravan of wagons
Hustled toward the big warehouses.

In response to their inquiries,
They were told the *River Ranger*
Had tied up at Towson Landing.

In the days of Great Raft trouble,
Only the most daring captains
Would attempt to bring their steamboats
Up Red River to the Landing.
Those who had the skill and fortune
To negotiate the hazards
Of the tricky river channel
Were rewarded with rich profits.

"How far is it to the landing?"
Newton asked. "Four miles," a soldier
Answered. "Let us go there, Randall,"
Newton said, and off they galloped.

"Why the big rush?" queried Randall.
"I was under the impression
You were bending every effort
To reach New Orleans in record
Time, but now you dillydally!"

"On the other hand," said Newton,

"I may gain some time by booking
Passage on the *River Ranger*."

"Never thought of that," said Randall.

After talking with the captain,
Newton was convinced that he could
Get to New Orleans much sooner
On the *Ranger*. He paid passage.

Captain Greer's announced intention
Of departing bright and early
On the morrow for New Orleans
Called for hurried preparation
On the part of several persons
Who had business in the city.
"What will you do with your horses?"
Randall asked. "I'll make arrangements
For them at the fort," said Newton.

After introductions, Newton
Told the commandant his story.

"Colonel Lovelace is an old friend,"
Said the major. "We will gladly
Make provisions for your horses.

"Sergeant Bailey will escort you
To your quarters. I shall expect
You and your friend at my table
In the mess hall. After supper
We will try our hands at poker.
In the morning, Sergeant Bailey
Will go with you to the Landing
And return your mount to Towson."

It was four A. M. when Newton
Said farewell to Randall Duncan
And departed for the Landing.

Big stern-wheeler, *River Ranger*,
With a head of steam, was ready
To depart when Newton cautioned
Bailey to take care of Beauty,
Turned and hurried up the gangway.

Other passengers included
Joseph Berthelet, a wealthy
French-Canadian Indian trader;
John Heald, a well-known cotton broker
Employed by a half-blood Choctaw,
Robert M. Jones, operator
Of a number of plantations;
Elias Boudinot, Junior,
Brilliant Cherokee attorney;
And Alvin Goode, a young Baptist
Missionary-educator.

"There is coffee in the galley,"
Captain Greer announced, "and breakfast
Will be served as soon as we have
Cleared the dock and start down river."

Newton introduced himself to
Several travelers who were near him.
After breakfast, as he started
Deckward, Givens was accosted
By a friendly, gray-haired, smiling
Gentleman of marked appearance:
"Berthelet's my name, young fellow.

From appearances, and newness
Of your uniform, I gather
You are new to Indian country."

"Newton Givens is my name, sir.
You are right in your deductions.
I am new to *all* this country.
Two days since I pledged allegiance
To America. I travel
To New Orleans on important
Business, after which my future
Lies in Indian Territory
And, eventually, in Texas."

IV

"In my humble estimation,
You have made a wise decision,"
Berthelet said. "There is no land
That compares with this great region.
I live in the Territory
Near Fort Towson, but I journey
On my trading expeditions
Into Texas. I have sometimes
Thought of moving there, but somehow
Roots sink deep as years roll onward
And the old associations
Pull me homeward like a magnet.

"When I first came to this country,
The flag of France flew above it.
I was ten years old; my father
Was a trapper-hunter-trader.

Eight years later, when he journeyed
Back to Montreal, I stayed here.
I have never known the slightest
Urge to leave. It's home. I love it.

"Please forgive me for becoming
Overly enthusiastic
When I talk about the country
That has nurtured me and given
So unstintingly of blessings.
I forget you are a stranger
And not interested in the
Reminiscences of oldsters—
You are looking toward the future."

"Every word that you have spoken
Has a deep appeal," said Newton.
"Knowledge of the past is needful
In one's planning for the future.
It would be a downright pleasure
And a privilege to listen
To your story of the region."

Flattered, Berthelet continued:
"Not long after our arrival
In this land, negotiations
Were completed for its purchase
From Napoleon who needed
Money to finance ambitious
Plans for war and world conquest.

"Eighteen Seventeen was witness
To construction of the parent
Frontier fortress of importance

In the land soon to be labeled
Territory of the Indians.

"In the pretty Ozark foothills,
Where the Arkansas and Poteau
Rivers join, a promontory,
Covered by wild ferns and flowers,
Was selected for location
Of Fort Smith, built for protection
Of white settlers from the red men.

"Seven years from Fort Smith's founding
Saw establishment of Towson,
And Fort Gibson, an important
Installation to the northward.
Washita, the farthest westward
Of the forts, is a newcomer—
It was built to speed advancement
Of the white man toward the sunset
And protect the Nations' members
From marauding South Plains Indians.

V

"I have watched the Territory
Change from a primeval region
To a land of healthy commerce.
Doaksville, my home, is a thriving
Village with some half a dozen
Trading posts, a wagon maker,
Gristmill, saddle shop, a hotel,
And a pretty whitewashed church house.

107

"Almost constant streams of pack trains
Come to Doaksville for their trade goods.
Bartering with wild Plains Indians
Is a lucrative profession
For adventurous bushrangers.

"Good plantations in increasing
Numbers dot the fertile valleys
Of the Arkansas and Big Red.

"During shipping season, landings
Are piled high with bales of cotton,
Beeswax, bear's grease, peltries — waiting
To be loaded for down-river
Trip to New Orleans and markets
In the North and East and Europe.

"By no means are all newcomers
To the frontier crude unlettered
Plainsmen clad in lowly buckskin.
Freedom and the chance of living
Fuller lives in newer countries
Call as clearly now as ever.
Aristocrats and pathfinders
Hear the call and many of them
Answer — they cannot resist it!

"I have met some of the greatest
Military men and others
Of our time. For instance, Irving,
One of our land's most distinguished
Men of letters came to Gibson
To hunt buffalo and study

The frontier and its advancement
Toward the faraway horizon.
And George Catlin, famous artist,
Lived at Scullyville while painting
Some of his most noted pictures.
It is true the Territory
Was established for the red man,
But the paleface also likes it!
Strangely, this has always happened
And I cannot help but wonder
How long it will take the white man
To possess the Territory—
'Permanent' home of the Indians . . . "

Chapter Eleven

The Five Nations

AT THE SUPPER table, Newton
Sat beside the young attorney,
Boudinot, who held attention
Of the diners as he chatted
Easily on current topics.

Next day, on deck, Givens seated
Himself by the lounging lawyer
And engaged in conversation:

"Last night at the supper table
You made mention of 'Five Nations,'
And I failed to grasp your meaning.
I could understand that Indians
Were referred to, but my knowledge
Of the race is very meager.
You see, I am a late comer
To America. My interest
In the tribes is, I assure you,
Quite sincere and I should like to,
If I may impose upon you,
Have you tell me of the Nations."

"That, my friend, will be a pleasure,
And it is no imposition.
I do not recall the reference
But 1 do possess abundant
Information on the Nations
And their conflicts with the white man.

II

"From beginning of colonial
Times the white man searched for methods
Of removing Indian neighbors
From immediate surroundings.
Purpose was twofold: the cultures
Of the races were in conflict;
Land was needed for expansion.

"Treaties were negotiated
As a rule to gain land cessions,
After which the displaced red men
Found new homes by moving onward.

"Dealings of this type were often
Marked by fraud, threats of reprisal,
Bribery, and as a final
Resort, whiskey, which robbed Indians
Of their reason, made them helpless
Pawns in hands of politicians.

"Following the Revolution,
Both state and federal governments
Made such treaties with the red men.
Early in the Eighteen Hundreds,
Legislation passed by Congress

Authorized the president to
Exchange lands which were included
In the Louisiana Purchase
For the lands of eastern Indians.

"Under this provision, some tribes,
Long relieved of their ancestral
Realms, were transferred to the new land.

"Eighteen Thirty legislation,
Named the Indian Removal Act,
Made provision for transplanting
All the tribes of eastern Indians
To 'Permanent Indian Country,'
West of Mississippi River,
Where, avowed the laws and treaties,
'Red men will not be molested
Until grass shall grow no longer,
And the waters cease their flowing.'

"Government proposals offered
Fifteen hundred acre headrights
To each male adult, plus monthly
Allotments of food and money.
In addition, transportation
To the new land would be furnished.
Full protection, too, was offered
From marauding wild Plains Indians.

III

"The Black Hawk War quickly ended
Opposition of the northern
Tribes. However, the Five Nations,

Living in the sunny Southland,
Cherokees, Chickasaws, Choctaws,
Creeks, and Seminoles resisted
The removal from their homelands.

"These tribes, civilized through contact
For two hundred years with white men,
Owned land in the Carolinas,
Georgia, Tennessee, Florida,
Mississippi, Alabama.

"Propaganda represented
That the Indian transplantation
Was a philanthropic gesture
On the part of governmental
Agencies and would redound to
Better living for the red men.
But the Indians well remember
It as one of the most evil
Deeds in all our country's history.

"Numbers of the southern tribesmen
Had become well educated,
Were slave-holders, operated
Fine plantations. The professions,
Legal, medical, and others,
Had attracted many of them.

"Well established in their homelands,
The Five Nations were persistent
In their fight against displacement.
But the strong desires of white men
Would not brook, for long, denial.

"Eighteen Thirty-two, the Choctaws,
First of Nations to surrender,
Sailed on steamboats up Red River
Toward the mouth of Kiamichi,
Their new home in Indian Country.

"Many miles from destination,
Steamboats, sadly overloaded,
Grounded and the hapless Choctaws
Had to leave their scant possessions
And march under harsh conditions
Through the tangled woods and marshes.

"Soon the Chickasaws were exiled;
Then removal reached a stalemate.

"Two years passed. The Seminoles, Creeks,
And Cherokees still rejected
All bids made to dispossess them.
Public sentiment in favor
Of the Indians started building
In New England and in other
Sections. The administration
Was embarrassed. Andrew Jackson
Was elected on a platform
Calling for the transplantation.

"Politicians started working
For establishment of Indian
Territory. Congress passed the
Act in Eighteen Thirty-four that
Sealed the fate of diehard Indians.

IV

"Seminoles took arms in defense
Of their domain. After seven
Years of conflict, costing fifteen
Hundred lives and some ten million
Dollars, they capitulated—
All except a few who escaped
To the Everglades. They're still there!

"Finally, the Creeks abandoned
Hope of holding their possessions.
Unseaworthy boats were marshaled
Into service to transport them;
Hundreds lost their lives in shipwrecks.
Hunger and starvation plagued them
On the journey to their new home.

"University-schooled lawyers
Of the Cherokees matched legal
Wits with government attorneys
Quite successfully for four years.
It appeared that legal action
Might drag on *ad infinitum*.

"To halt further delay, orders
Were issued instructing General
Winfield Scott to take an army
Of two thousand men and force the
Indians to the Territory.

"All in all, the way was bloody—
'Trail of Tears,' Cherokees call it.
The march was an Indian epic

Of tragedy and inhuman
Hardship wantonly inflicted.

"By late Eighteen Thirties, sixty
Thousand members of the Nations
Were transplanted. Many million
Acres of the finest farm land
In the Southland passed to white men.

"Fortunately, the Five Nations
Made adjustments in fine order.
Today we are running cattle,
Raising cotton, trapping, trading,
Forging new lives in a new land."

"Thank you," Newton said. "Your story
Has, indeed, been most revealing.
Mine had been a false impression
That mentality of Indians
Hovered near the savage level.
I must make some readjustments
In my concept of your people."

V

. . . Alvin Goode, the missionary,
Closed his Bible, smiled and nodded
A good morning: "Had your coffee?"

"No," said Newton, "let me join you.
I would like some information.
Sometime back, while I was talking
With young Boudinot he told me
Of the high regard his people
Hold for you, and of your efforts

To enhance their living standard.
I am interested in learning
How the missionary movement
Started in the Territory."

"In reality it started
Long before the Indians came here,"
Goode said, warming to the subject.

"Presbyterian and Baptist
Missionaries, who converted
Many of them in their homelands,
Followed the Five Nations westward.
They were well advanced in farming,
Government, religion, schooling.
We were fearful lest they revert
To their former savage customs
In the face of shabby treatment
At the hands of their white brothers.
But the facts are: intermarriage
With the Scotch and English traders
And the consequent up-breeding,
Plus their long association
With white people has convinced them
That they must continue climbing
Toward a better life and culture
Or be lost in mad confusion
Of the internecine struggle
That is decimating many
Other tribes who are unwilling
Or incapable of making
The adjustments necessary
To compete and live with white men.

"In the old days they were happy
Living on the golden bounty
Of an all-providing nature.
Mayhap, they would rather perish
Than accept the ways of white men—
Sometimes one can hardly blame them!

"Long since, members of the Nations
Organized a constitutional
Form of government. Their children
Go to mission schools. They worship
The same God that white men worship.

"Baptists operate a growing
Mission school of higher learning
At Bokchito, in the heart of
Choctaw country, west of Doaksville.

"Many tribesmen are quite skilled in
Greek and Latin, while some traders
Cannot write their names. Ironic?

"Indian efforts toward the better
Life are certainly praiseworthy.
I believe that the Five Nations
Will, with half a chance, develop
Into citizens deserving
Of the high regard of all men.

" . . . I enjoyed the coffee, Givens,
I must go and do some packing.
"We'll be docking late this evening."

Chapter Twelve

Warm Welcome

JEB, THE melancholy butler,
Shed his stiffness as he greeted
Newton: "Sir, it's good to see you.
Miss Lucinda's been so lonely!
She is in the Old French Parlor;
Follow, I will take you to her."

As they neared the room, a love song
Floated down the hall to greet them.
Through an open door he saw her,
Gowned in lovely turquoise satin,
Playing the pianoforte.

Jeb discreetly turned and left him.
Newton listened for a moment
Then walked quietly behind her,
Bent and kissed her titian tresses.

"Oh, my darling!" cried Lucinda.
"Only God knows how I missed you!"

Newton pressed her to his bosom,
Telling her how much he loved her.
When the long embrace was over,
He inquired about the family.

119

"Mama and the twins are having
Supper at the Chalmettes. Somehow,
I felt certain you would be here
Tonight, though your letter stated
You would not arrive till Friday.
You are a full five days early.
And, my dearest, I'm too happy
To inquire how it was managed—
All that counts is, we're together!"

Newton told her of the changing
Of his plans, and how the *Ranger*
"Sped me homeward to my darling!"

"Mama has been in a dither
For two weeks now," said Lucinda,
"But the wedding preparations
Have gone nicely. Grand-Mere DuPuy
Wrote that she and Jacque are
Coming. They'll be here tomorrow.
Ah, that Edwin might be present!
And if Papa does not get here,
I shall be sore disappointed."

As they chatted, Jeb approached them
To say that the Lovelace carriage
Had just turned into the driveway.

Madame Lovelace welcomed Newton
With a hearty, cordial greeting.
Annette and Nanette talked gaily
Of the wedding plans. Quipped Nanette,
"It shall be a grand occasion,

One that even gay and wicked
New Orleans will long remember!"
Madame Lovelace frowned in horror,
Shushing further conversation.

. . . Madame Lovelace and Lucinda
The twins, Grand-Mere, and the seamstress
Worked at finalizing details
Of the trousseau and the wedding.

II

Uncle Jacque and Newton, finding
Time upon their hands, were walking
Through the Vieux Carre admiring
Scenes that came to their attention:
Black-robed nuns beside the convent
Fingered rosaries and listened
To the drone of children's voices
As in unison they murmured
Pious verses from the Scriptures.

From the eaves of weathered tiling
Pigeons cooed a doleful chorus.
Slaves, half-naked and perspiring,
Bearing heavy-laden baskets
On their heads, walked toward the market.

Noontime found them near the portals
Of the great Hotel St. Louis.
"Here the Louisiana gumbo
Is a food for gods," said Uncle
Jacque. "It was originated
In the famed St. Louis kitchens.
Let us enter and enjoy some."

121

When the savory meal was finished,
They walked into the Rotunda,
A large circular apartment
With a spacious high-domed ceiling,
Where a scene of human bondage
Was unfolding. Spellbound, Newton
Watched as slaves of all descriptions
Were sold to the highest bidders.
Darky after darky parted
Company with his companions.

III

One, a well-proportioned creature,
Was the center of attention.
"In his native land," mused Newton,
"He would surely have been ruler
Of his tribe. His princely bearing
Marks him as one born a leader."

Newton heard a Creole planter
Whisper to his overseer:
"He's the one that I was telling
You about, and I am willing
To pay fifteen hundred dollars,
Which is more than twice the figure
He is worth at going prices.
Understand? I want that nigger—
He can do the work of three slaves."

Placed upon the block, the ebon
Study in physique gazed sadly
At the crowd. His eyes found Newton's:

In the eloquence of silence
Newton felt an urgent message:
"Buy me, Mistah! Help me! Save me
From ignominy of bondage."

Loud the auctioneer proclaimed that
"He's a natural-born musician,
Golden-voiced and plays the fiddle
With the deft touch of a master.
He has worked in fields and households,
On the wharves and on the steamboats—
He is one slave in a thousand
Who is worthy of his upkeep!
Start your bidding. Make it lively!
He will bring a handsome figure!"

"I will bid five hundred dollars,
As a starter," said a buxom
Woman dressed in lace and satin.

"Who will make it seven-fifty?"
Asked the auctioneer. Excitement
Grew as bidding passed a thousand.

Finally, at fifteen hundred,
Bidding slowed. Again the pleading
Eyes were gazing hard at Newton.
He could not refrain from saying,
"I will bid two thousand dollars!"

"Going once, and twice, and three times,"
Said the auctioneer. "You bought him."

"Strike his shackles!" Newton ordered.

As they dropped from off his ankles,
Silence fell in the Rotunda.

"Write him out a bill of freedom,"
Newton told the clerk. The awestruck
Crowd looked on in wide-eyed wonder,
As did David faced with freedom.

Feelingly the Negro stammered,
"Ah is grateful beyon' measuah . . .
But Ah cannot accep' freedom . . .
Ah ain't got no place to put it.
Only let me do yoah biddin' . . .
Yoah will find me mighty faithful."

Newton handed him the papers,
But he pleaded: "Suh, yoah keep 'em."

"Very well, but they will always
Be yours — any time you want them . . . "

IV

Afternoon before the wedding,
Newton, walking by the river
Where a steamboat was unloading,
Heard the voice of Colonel Lovelace:
"Well, my boy, you came to meet me!"

"Frankly, I did not expect you,"
Newton said, "but I am happy
That you are here. Madame Lovelace
And the girls will be delighted."

V

Newton and Lucinda married
In the spacious Lovelace drawing
Room when slowly falling shadows

Blended into purple twilight.
Candles shed a glow of magic
O'er the altar as they plighted
Troths in solemn ceremony.

Fair Lucinda's fragile beauty
Was accentuated by her
Bridal gown of ivory satin.
Down the sleeves were tiers of ruffles;
Pearl embroidery graced the neck line.
Her illusion veil cascaded
From a coronet of pearls.
Her bouquet was snow-white roses.

In the dining room a festive
Spirit reigned as all the party
Entered into merrymaking.

The massive cut glass chandelier
Held a hundred flaming candles,
Casting a rich glow on crystal
Goblets and the polished silver
Placed in order on the table
For the gala wedding banquet.

VI

Later, as they danced cotillions,
Newton whispered to Lucinda:
"Am I dreaming, or is Edwin
Standing in the doorway watching?"

"Edwin! Edwin!" cried Lucinda,
Rushing forth to greet her brother.

As she kissed his cheek and hugged him,
She drew back in shocked amazement!
"Sis, I need a drink," said Edwin.
Then he fell dead-drunk beside her.

Colonel Lovelace, stunned and shaken,
Called to Jeb to carry Edwin
To his room, then turned and hurried
To his wife and tried to comfort
Her with words of soft assurance:
"Though we cannot understand this,
It will all be well tomorrow."

Two days later, after treatment
By the family physician,
Edwin broke the alcoholic
Stupor long enough to tell them
Of the piracy committed
Near a bandit-ridden island
Somewhere in the far Pacific:
He had lost his ship and fortune.

"I will fill you in on details
Later. Let me rest," said Edwin.

"It is obvious," the doctor
Said, "that he has quite a problem.
He has been inebriated
For some time and it is doubtful
That the habit can be broken."

Wednesday Edwin showed improvement
And the colonel was insistent

That the newlyweds continue
With their plans for honeymooning.

VII

When the steamboat *Mary Arden*
Sailed for Natchez, they were on board
Headed for The Oaks plantation
And an interlude of blissful
Days before they started westward
To the fort in Indian country.
Overhead a burnished copper
Moon spilled magic over all the
Earth, and Newton and Lucinda
Leaned against the rail enraptured.

Looking at the moon's reflection
In the water, Newton murmured:
"Once that same moon cast entrancing
Spells upon the Nile in springtime;
Antony and Cleopatra
Felt it, and their love was heightened.

"On a South Sea isle a native
Prince in ages long departed
Pressed the lips of pretty virgins
As the moon smiled down upon them.
And tonight it splashes its charm
Over you and me, my darling:
But of all the countless lovers
Who have known its conjuration,
Not one ever felt the mighty
Power of its spell as I do

When I feel your racing heart beat
Answer mine, my dear Lucinda.
It invokes a solemn promise:
In the morning of our marriage,
I shall sing my ardent love song;
Each day I shall add new verses,
And the song shall not be ended
Until I can sing no longer.
I shall sing my blithesome heart out,
Capture time's imagination,
Mold it into an eternal
Song of love without an ending.

"Aye, I pledge thee love unending—
Constant as the stars that shineth
From the lofty heights of heaven . . .
Winds that kiss the highest mountains
Symbolize the fond affection
I shall ever shower upon you.
Like the love of prairie flowers
For the rich green earth that nurtures
Them and loves them for their brightness,
Thus shall be my love encircling
Thee in bonds of tender twining.
. . . Love, Lucinda sweet, is boundless!"

Quietly Lucinda answered:
"You are right, dear, love is boundless.
I have always known full certain
I would give my heart to someone
Who would give it back rich laden,
Filled to brimming, running over

With the love so fondly given!
Like bread cast upon the waters,
Love one gives away returneth
Greatly increased, warmly tender,
And demanding to be given
Endlessly to form a circle
Rising upward toward the apex
Of the universe and heaven."

Chapter Thirteen

Trip to Washita

WHEN THE honeymoon was over,
Newton and Lucinda started
To Fort Washita. At Natchez
Antoine Prudhomme told Lucinda
He had talked with Colonel Lovelace
In New Orleans. He had said that
He was taking Edwin with him
To the Indian Territory.

"Ed's compulsive urge for liquor,"
Prudhomme had continued sadly,
"Must be broken if he ever
Is to draw another sober
Breath. I swear he has the habit!"

When the steamboat *Golden Eagle*
Docked at Natchez they were ready
With their luggage and the other
Items they were taking with them
To add comfort to their quarters
At Fort Washita. When good-byes
Were said to their friends the Prudhommes
And the others of the little

Group who came to wish a pleasant
Journey to them, they departed.

Trip to Fort Smith was delightful
Through a world of many-splendored
Riverscapes that left them breathless.

II

Upon inquiry at Fort Smith,
Newton learned that Josiah Doak
Planned to leave next day for Doaksville,
Where he was an Indian trader.

"Yes, sir, we'll be glad to take you,"
Said Josiah. "We'll be leaving
When we get the wagons loaded.
Noon tomorrow we'll be ready."

"Sir, I really planned," said Newton,
"To hire a teamster and wagon,
Since I have so much equipment—
Furniture and trunks and bedding."

Said Josiah, "I've been needing
One more wagon. I'll just buy it.
Go and get your stuff together."

III

Brilliant panoramas stretching
Into wonderlands of beauty
Kept Lucinda in high spirits.

"Are you happy?" Newton asked her.

131

"Yes, I could go on forever
Savoring the keen excitement
Of not knowing what is hidden
Beyond hills that stretch before us."

And Lucinda's eyes were starry
As she added, "But whatever
Lies out there, we'll share together—
This is happiness like heaven's!"

Five days later as they traveled
Down the military roadway,
They came to an intersection
With the Texas Road. Josiah
Pointed toward a nearing dust cloud:
"Longhorns coming! Plenty of 'em!"

Doak soon led his train of wagons
To a knoll beside the roadway
To permit some eighteen hundred
Longhorn cattle with their drovers
To pass. They were travel-weary.
And took little or no notice
Of the wagons headed southward.

IV

When the trail boss drew abreast them,
Doak exclaimed, "It's Toby Larkin!"

"Well, Josiah, hit's been ages
Since I seen yu! Wher' yu goin'?"

"Doaksville," Doak said, "Where I saw you
Last, six years ago — or seven?"

"Hit's been seven," Larkin answered.
"Time slips by like speedin' lightnin'.
I have saw a lot o' water
Flow downstream since last I seen yu."

"That's the biggest herd of cattle
Ere I've seen come through the Nations,"
Said Josiah, "Where'd they come from?"

"Goliad, in southern Texas,"
Larkin said, and added wryly:
"We hev trailed them bawlin' buzzards
Five long months and Baxter Springs is
Still a month away. Sedalia
Is still farther. I'll be happy
When the long ol' drive is done with!"

When the cloven hooves no longer
Sounded and the dust was settling,
Larkin said good-by and started
In an easy lope behind them.

V

"Really, I had no idea
That there were so many longhorns
In the country," said Lucinda,
As the wagons rumbled onward.

"Parts of Texas teem with longhorns,"
Said Josiah. "Now that markets
Are established, herds that travel
Texas Road grow ever larger."

"It is obvious," said Newton,

Where they got their name, but tell me,
Are they indigenous to Texas?"

"No," Josiah said, "the Spaniards
Brought a wealth of bovine-equine
Life to Mexico soon after
Cortes conquered Montezuma's
Rich domain. The Andalusian
Cattle multiplied and prospered.
In a decade the vast valleys
Of the land were overflowing
With the hardy long-horned cattle.

"With expansion of the Spanish
Conquest northward into Texas
And New Mexico the cattle,
Never too tame, soon were roaming
Wild in some parts of the country.

"*Haciendas* and huge ranches
Gradually became a pattern
In the realm of southern Texas
And the land assumed the nickname
"Rawhide State" because the cattle
Were as vital to the Texan
As were buffaloes to Indians.

"Longhorns are much more than cattle
To the cowman down in Texas:
They are hide and horn and candle,
Medium of exchange, breakfast,
Dinner, supper, soap, fat, harness,
Saddles, saddlebags and gun slings;
They are lariats and bull whips.

They are cradles for the babies
And the very bed he sleeps on.
From the hides he weaves chair bottoms,
Fashions doors for home and dugout,
Carpets for his floors and pictures
For the walls are burned in rawhide.

"When a market came for cattle,
They had to make a road to get them
To the towns and market places—
That's how come the Texas Road built.

"The Texas Road has adapted
Portions of the old Shawnee
Trail and Osage Trace, long traveled
By the red man. Now it stretches
From Forth Worth to Kansas City.
From Red River to the Kansas
Line it passes through lands owned by
Members of the Five Great Nations.

"Some two years ago, the Texans
Started driving longhorn cattle
Up to Baxter Springs in Kansas,
And Sedalia in Missouri—
Some go on to Kansas City.

"Cherokees, the Creeks, and Choctaws,
Realizing that the trail herds
Were tréspassing on their domains,
Figured that they could do better
Than accept the scrawny stragglers
Drovers gave them for the passage
Of the cattle through the Nations.

135

"Soon a tollgate was erected
At Limestone Gap on the headright
Of Charles Leflore, Choctaw leader.
The gap is a natural gateway
To a great time-saving short-cut
Through the Limestone Hills. A payment
Of ten cents a head was set by
Leflore as the price for passage.

"Drovers raised a howl of protest,
But they paid the toll. Soon other
Tribes also demanded payment.
Choctaws raised the price to fifty
Cents per head. The Creeks did likewise.
Seventy-five cents is charged by
Cherokees. These prices added
To the fees of the inspectors,
Ferry payments, and the losses
Naturally incurred in trail drives,
May put cowmen out of business,
But right now the trail is lively."

VI

Sunday Josiah commented:
"To reach Doaksville by tomorrow
We must drive all night; I'm sorry,
But I must not disappoint the
Choctaws — they will be there waiting.
Their annuities are due them.
Rations must be issued Monday,
And the rations are included
In the merchandise we carry

On the wagon train . . . You see, then,
It's imperative we get there."

"Do not mind me," smiled Lucinda,
"I think that will be exciting!"

"Fine," said Newton. "We can stand it."

VII

. . . Night came slowly, diamond studded,
Velvet-gowned, a lovely lady,
Arms outstretched to the horizon,
Searching with her eager fingers
For another gem of splendor—
An adornment for her tresses.

There emerged a giant ruby
Of a moon . . . the lady placed it
At a most becoming angle
In her hair. She kicked her shoes off,
Settled back in admiration
Of her bejeweled reflection
In Lucinda's eyes . . . And Newton
Hummed a love song as they journeyed
Down the silvery trail to Doaksville.

VIII

Dawn was peaking over eastern
Hills when they rolled into Doaksville.
Several thousand Choctaw Indians
Camped within a square mile's distance
Of the trading post Josiah

Operated with his partner,
Vinson Timms, who came from Ireland.

Cabins, tents and booths and shanties,
Ambulances, carts and wagons
Overflowed with motley humans,
Red and black and white and mixtures
In every shade and proportion.
Even at the early dawning
They were "buying, selling, swapping;
Betting, shooting, strutting, talking;
Laughing, fiddling, eating, drinking;
Smoking, sleeping, seeing . . . being
Seen, all huddled close together." *

Newton and Lucinda spent the
Morning resting. After dinner
They continued with another
Driver assigned by Josiah
Toward Fort Washita. The heavens
Smiled upon them as they traveled.

IX

At Fort Washita the neighbors
Helped them rearrange their quarters
To accommodate the pretty
Items they had brought from Natchez.
When the work was all completed,
Newton and Lucinda's quarters
Were the envy of the outpost.

---

* **Description by Alvin Goode, Indian Archives, Oklahoma Historical Society.**

Next, housewarming was in order:
Officers and wives joined forces
In extending cordial welcome
To "the misery that glitters
At Fort Washita and other
Army posts along the frontier,"
As the wife of Major Marlowe
Called the life that they were joining.

X

Two weeks after their arrival,
Newton and Lucinda greeted
Colonel Lovelace, who, with Edwin,
Arrived on the stage from Towson.
Colonel Lovelace was discouraged;
He could not keep Edwin sober.
"How he manages for liquor
Is beyond me!" sighed the colonel.

As the days sped by, the tranquil
Grassy slopes and swaying leafy
Trees turned from an avocado
Green to brown and taffy color.
It was fall and ere long snowflakes
Kissed the earth, announcing winter.

At the spinning wheel, Lucinda
Turned out tiny strips of homespun
Which she dyed with dazzling colors
She acquired from Choctaw Indians.

With a span of mules and wagon
Borrowed from the quartermaster,

139

Newton brought a load of laurel
And a tree of shapely cedar
From the bluffs along the river.

Christmas found the Givens parlor
Warm and cozy with the tree dressed
In the brightly streaming ribbands
And festoons of colored popcorn.
Dips of tallow used for lighting,
Added warmth and cheer and comfort
To the hearts of those who viewed it:
Soldiers brave and gentle women
Who had come to test their mettle
On the grim realities of
Life in outposts of the army.

On the last day of December
Orders came for Colonel Lovelace
And Newton Givens to join the
Staff of officers at Towson.

Chapter Fourteen

Little Newton

ON A CLEAR brisk morn in winter,
When the scintillating sunshine
Spilled its warming beams of glory
Over hill and dale, Lucinda
Said she would prepare a picnic
Lunch. "If you will saddle horses,
We can go to High-Hill Lookout.
It's a perfect day for riding."

"What a wonderful suggestion!"
Exclaimed Newton. "Count me present."

When the crest was reached, a blanket
Served as resting place and table.
Following their lunch, the couple
Stretched out side by side. Lucinda
Nestled her head on his shoulder.

"Darling," she said, "a confession
Is in order. I persuaded
You to come here through deception.
Truly, I enjoyed the picnic,
But I brought you here to tell you
That you are to be a father."

"Ah, my sweetheart," murmured Newton.
"I have been in seventh heaven
Ever since the day I wed you.
Now the brimming cup of marriage
Runneth over. Sweet Lucinda,
I am happiest of all men!
On the crest of High-Hill Lookout
We are sitting, drenched in sunshine,
On a mountain top of marvels."

II

. . . March came in a roaring lion
And Lucinda was becoming,
Day by day, more wan and restless.

Apprehensive, Newton watched her,
Talked with Edwin and the colonel,
And consulted the post doctor.

Dr. Sullivan, post surgeon,
Whose advice was most uncertain,
Was adept at amputating
Mangled limbs of wounded soldiers,
But had never once attended
One whose footsteps soon would carry
Her across the shadowed threshold
Into motherhood and secrets
Shared alone by God and mothers.

Newton's gentle care and efforts
To assure her of well-being,
Left her unresponsive, moody.
He decided that she needed
The attention of her mother
And the twins and Grand-Mere Du Puy.

With assistance of the colonel,
Newton talked her into going
Home to New Orleans, and Edwin
Said he would be glad to take her.

"Can we trust you to stay sober?"
Asked the colonel. You are doing
Quite well with your drinking problem,
But I never know for certain
If you will be drunk or sober."

"I'll stay sober," Edwin answered.
"That's a promise. I'll stay sober
Until we get to New Orleans."

Newton learned upon inquiry
That the *Belle of Crescent City*
Would be leaving Scully Landing
Bright and early Sunday morning.

Scullyville was fairly teeming—
Saturdays were always busy—
When the Givens party got there.

At the inn they left instructions
To be called at three in order
To be present at the Landing
When the steamboat left at sunrise.

Daybreak, heartbreak for Lucinda,
Found them nearing Scully Landing.
Soon the heavy trunk was loaded;
Fond farewells were said. The *Crescent*
Started downstream and Lucinda
Waved until the bending river

143

Took him from her sight. Then Newton
Climbed into the carriage heading,
Heavy-hearted, toward Fort Towson.

III

. . . "I am going back," Lucinda
Sobbed. "I simply cannot stand it!"

Edwin, master of persuasion,
Tried to comfort her, assuring
That "Fort Towson is no proper
Place for you to have your baby.
Sensitive, aristocratic
Ladies certainly were never
Meant to bear the brutish burdens
Of a frontier post. This country
Must be tamed by seasoned soldiers.
It is wild and fierce, unconquered—
And unfit for well-bred ladies."

"Edwin," said Lucinda gently,
"Everywhere that history traces
Patterns with harsh trails and human
Hardship, women follow husbands
With endurance, patience, courage
And the will to ever bolster
Them and help them in their struggle.
It is true new lands are conquered
By the men — it is their challenge;
But the job of civilizing
New domains is in the province
Of what you term 'well-bred ladies'—

And it is the greater challenge!
Theirs will always be the truly
Difficult role on the trying
Stage of moving frontier action."

Passengers, at first struck speechless,
Joined Edwin in persuasion.
Their entreaties fell on deaf ears:
For the picture of a lonely
Handsome soldier sadly, waving
From the barren bank behind her
Could not be erased. Lucinda
Sat upon her trunk demanding
That the captain turn the *Crescent*
Upstream — back to Scully Landing.

Captain Martin grinned, explaining
He would like to do her bidding,
But he could not turn the *Crescent*
As the channel was too narrow.

"And," he said, "I have a schedule;
I am duty-bound to keep it.
We will meet the *Southern Rover*
At Fort Smith, and if you care to,
You may take it back to Scully."

"I am going back to Towson,"
She insisted. "Whither Newton
Goest, I go. I belong there!
In the short time spent at Towson
I have learned to love the open
Spaces and the sound of soldiers
On the drill ground and the constant

Hoofbeats pounding down the roadway,
And the groan of laden wagons
Bringing in supplies, equipment.
Reveille and taps are music
To my ears. The sun-down cannon
Tells me all is well at Towson.
And . . . I even love the Indians!
They are interesting and worthy
Of support by all right-thinking
People — though so few admit it!"

As the *Crescent* neared the mooring
At Fort Smith, the *Southern Rover*
Headed toward the river channel.
Captain Martin signaled to her,
And she pulled back to the dock-side.

After hurried explanations,
Edwin and Lucinda boarded,
And the huge stern-wheeler started
Upstream — and to Scully Landing.

IV

. . . When the *Rover*, some time later,
Tied up at the Landing, Newton
Sprang on deck with arms extended,
And Lucinda flew into them.

"I was halfway back to Towson,"
Newton laughed, "when something told me
You'd be back. I came to meet you!"

Arm in arm they left the *Rover*.

146

Edwin, busy with unloading
Of the trunk and other baggage,
Slowly shook his head and muttered:
"I'll be danged if they're not psychic!
I am going to get some whiskey
And forget all earthly problems."

Edwin was sot drunk when Newton
Gently placed him in the carriage.

Life at Towson took on added
Luster as spring turned to summer.

V

Little Newton came to join them
On their wedding anniversary.
First child born to an officer's
Family at Towson, his birth
Was an event long remembered.

All the officers were gathered
To assist in the delivery
By proposing toasts and drinking—
Lustily and all too often—
To the health of Newton Givens.

The white women were assisted
By a lively delegation
Of squaws from the Choctaw Nation,
Who brought in a papoose cradle.

For the youngster's bath, a well-scrubbed
Tub that once held pickled mackerel
Was produced by thoughtful neighbors.

147

After he was bathed and swaddled,
The cooing squaws gently placed him
In the cradle, laced it snugly,
Soothed him into fitful slumber,
Placed him on the dining table
And departed in high spirits.

Colonel Lovelace, chest expanded,
Led the proud unsteady father
In to view his ruddy first-born.

Newton's eyes shone with a tender
Look of deep appreciation
As he gazed upon the sleeping
Child. "His hair is red," he murmured.
"I must now go to Lucinda."

"Dear, I am completely happy,"
Smiled Lucinda as he kissed her.

Chapter Fifteen

Edwin's Disappearance

EDWIN'S DRINKING problem worsened;
He was hardly ever sober.
Newton and Lucinda pleaded
With him to forsake his boozing,
But their pleas were never heeded.
Colonel Lovelace raged and threatened
To disown him — all was useless.

Newton's slave, the loyal David,
Was assigned as his companion.

On the twenty-third of August
Clayton Adams of St. Joseph,
With a guide and a surveyor,
Stopped at Fort Towson en route to
Santa Fe. He sought a short cut
From his home town in Missouri
To the prosperous trading center
In New Mexico. A fortune
Waited for the man who figured
Out a quicker way to get there
Than the old Trail long since traveled
Southwest out of Independence.

Edwin, hearing Clayton talking
With the colonel of his venture,
Planned to join the Adams party:
"Rid myself of all this nagging,"
Was the way that Edwin put it.

Taking Beauty, Newton's race horse,
And an Army pack mule laden
With provisions, bed roll, whiskey,
Edwin bribed a willing sentry
Not to mention his departure.

Two miles from the fort he waited
Until daybreak. Shortly Adams
And his men made their appearance.
Edwin, in beguiling manner,
Easily persuaded Adams
That the colonel would not question
His decision to go with him.

II

In midafternoon the guide said:
"I believe that we are followed;
I suspected it this morning.
It is my suggestion, Adams,
That we wait in yonder woodland
And determine who is spying
On our actions . . . could be trouble."

As they waited in the cover
Of the oak trees, Edwin ventured:
"I can see it is my shadow
Who approaches. My man David

Hardly ever lets me wander
Far beyond his line of vision.
Though a slave, he is devoted
To my welfare. This was one time
I was sure I had escaped him,
But I underestimated
His ability to follow.

"Hey, there, David, over this way!
You may join us. You'll be useful
Helping mark the trail we're blazing."

"Yassuh, yassuh, Mistah Edwin!
Ah is also good at cookin'."

Laughter greeted David's answer,
And his services were welcomed.

III

. . . Back at Towson, Colonel Lovelace
Fumed at Edwin's disappearance:
"Now he is a thief . . . He's stolen
Beauty and the mule and David,
Not to mention seven gallons
Of the Army's best-grade liquor!
I shall send a posse for him!"

"Wait a day or so," said Newton,
"He will probably return." But
Doubt was mirrored on his features.

IV

Ten days later all the colonel's
Fury turned to grief and worry.

Parties from Fort Smith were questioned,
But they had not seen the twosome.

"I assumed that they would head for
New Orleans but now it looks like
I was wrong. There is no telling
Where they are, or what has happened
To them. Is it possible that
They could have joined the Adams party?"

"I had thought of that," said Newton,
"Edwin sometimes talked of going
To New Mexico, but never
Did I think he really meant it."

V

As they talked some friendly Indians
Came into the fort and asked for
Lone Coyote . . . "We have journeyed,"
Said their spokesman "from direction
Of the sunset. Five sleeps backward
On the trail a man named David
Asked us to be sure to tell you
He and Edwin are with Adams."

Lone Coyote took the message
To the colonel. "Bring their chieftain
To my quarters," said the colonel.

After being reassured
All was well, the colonel ordered
That the Indians be rewarded
With a large supply of rations.

"Newton, would you and Coyote
Go to Santa Fe and get them?"
Queried beaming Colonel Lovelace.

"It will be a pleasure, Colonel,"
Newton said. Coyote nodded.

They had little difficulty
Following the trail that Adams
Marked with stones and stakes and blazes.

As they started Newton stated:
"Lone Coyote, I would like to
Master the Comanche language."

"Good," Coyote said. "I'll teach you.
On this trip our conversation
Shall be only in Comanche."

VI

In Santa Fe, Newton questioned
The innkeeper and was told that
Adams had been "gone a week now.
Joined a train of empty wagons
Bound for home in Independence."

"Was a man named Edwin Lovelace
With him?" Newton asked the keeper.

"Lovelace came here with the party
But he only stayed a couple
Of days. I have no idea
Where he went . . . and Mr. Adams
Looked for him but could not find him."

153

Givens searched the town but found no
Trace of Edwin. Late that evening
Two men came into the lobby
Of the inn and asked for lodging.
As they started to their quarters,
Newton glanced up recognizing
Robert Bent. As he approached him,
Hand extended, Robert exclaimed,
"Newton Givens! Well, I never
Dreamed I'd see you in this country!
This is Dan King, an employee
At the Fort. We've been to Taos."

"What a pleasure," Newton answered.
"I have thought of you quite often
And the fine association
We enjoyed at the fortress."

"Let me freshen up," said Robert.
"You must be my guest at supper."

At the supper table Newton
Told his friend about his mission.
"I am sadly disappointed,"
Givens said, "I fear we've lost them."

"No, you haven't" Robert told him.
"On our way here we encountered
Two men, one of whom was colored,
Who inquired the way to Taos.
I was positive I had seen
The horse ridden by the white man,
But till now I could not place it—

It was the mount you were riding
When you were at Bent's Fort last year.

"When you get to Taos, Kit Carson—
He and Charles married sisters—
Will be glad to lend assistance."

VII

At Taos, Carson's house was pointed
Out to Newton and he rode there.

Mr. Carson greeted Givens
With a warm and friendly handshake.

"I am Newton Givens. Searching
For a man named Edwin Lovelace;
With him is a slave called David.
I was told that you might help me.
This is my guide, Lone Coyote."

"Yes, we all know Edwin Lovelace
And the slave he calls his shadow.
He has been here several days now,
Living on a steady diet
Of Taos Lightning. It would kill me.
But it does not seem to bother
Mr. Lovelace. We have wondered
Where he came from and what motive
Could induce a man to drink so.
He is likeable and many
People here have tried to help him
Sober up, but he won't let them.

"Come to think of it, I have not
Seen him in a couple of days,
But I feel that he is nearby
As his mounts were in the livery
Barn this morning when I stopped there.

"Jim," called Carson, "do you know where
Edwin Lovelace is this evening?"

From another room Jim Bridger
Answered, "No, sir, but I saw him
In the barroom yesternoontide."

"Can you come in here a minute?"
Carson called again and Bridger
Shortly put in an appearance.

"This is Newton Givens, Bridger,
He is looking for Ed Lovelace."

"Pleased to meet you," nodded Bridger,
With a ham-like fist extended.
Newton gripped his hand explaining,
"Edwin Lovelace is an in-law,
I am married to his sister.
He left Towson Fort in August
Drunk, and both of us have worried
Ourselves sick. In desperation
I have searched the country over.
Friday Robert Bent informed me
That a man of his description,
With a slave for his companion,
Stopped him on the trail inquiring
How to get to Taos. He told him."

"Where did you see Robert?" Carson

Asked. "In Santa Fe," said Newton.
"I became acquainted with him
Last year when I was at Bent's Fort.
He insisted that I see you,
And that you could probably help me.
He informed me of his visit
Here in Taos. And he told me
That you and his brother Charles
Married sisters; make your homes here."

"Send your horses to the stable,"
Carson said. "And after supper
We shall make a few inquiries.
I am certain we will find him."

Following a hearty supper,
Givens, Carson, and Jim Bridger
Visited saloons in search of
Edwin, but they did not find him.

Charles Bent, whom they encountered
In the plaza, told them he had
Noticed Edwin walking southward,
Followed closely by the black man,
Toward the ranches in the valley
At an early evening hour.

"It grows late," said Carson, "let us
Get some sleep and in the morning
We will find them, be assured!"

VIII

On the morrow, bright and early,
Givens, Bridger, Bent, and Carson

And the loyal Lone Coyote
Headed for *Ranchos de Taos*,
Three miles southward from the village.

All day long they searched the ranches—
Looked in vain. Their eager question,
"Have you seen two strangers?" always
Brought responses: "*No, senores.*"

"I am heartsick," Newton murmured
As the sun was sinking westward.
"I was so sure we would find him.
Now it seems my hopes were groundless.
I can never tell Lucinda
That I could not find her brother."

Bridger offered the suggestion:
"Mayhap, he ran out of whiskey
And has gone back to the village."

"No," said Carson, "my instructions
To Josefa were that she should
Send a messenger if Edwin
Did return. I know he hasn't."

"Governor, have you a comment?"
Carson asked. "No, none whatever,"
Bent replied. "My disappointment
Knows no bounds. I, too, felt certain
That our quest would be rewarded."

"What do you think, Lone Coyote?"
Newton asked. The old guide answered:
"Inasmuch as no one saw them,
I suppose they did not come here.

I am fearful they have wandered
Out beyond the safety limits,
And they may be lost forever."

Carson offered this solution:
"Let us go back to the village.
In the morning searching parties
Shall be sent in all directions.
If they are alive, we'll find them."

IX

Passing by the pretty mission
Of Saint Francis de Assisi,
Home-bound searchers heard a greeting:
"Mistah Newton! I declah, Suh!
Is Ah evah glad to see yuh!
Look in yondah, Mistah Edwin's
Sobah as a jedge, so he'p me!"

David pointed through the gateway
Toward the altar of the mission
Where the weary Edwin rested.
Close beside him sat a *padre*,
Urging him to drink the coffee
He had brought him from his quarters.

"Edwin! Edwin!" Newton shouted,
"How I've hunted for you, fellow!
Oh, how good it is to find you!"

"I am sorry, Newton, sorry
For the trouble I have caused you . . .
For the grief I brought my parents
And my sisters; please forgive me.
I was led here in a drunken

159

Stupor . . . brought here for a purpose.
It has been a year . . . or longer
Since I have been truly sober.
I had lost my will for living—
Now a new one has been granted.
I am sure the Savior nodded
When I asked Him for forgiveness.
And He smiled . . . A weight was lifted
From my shoulders . . . I was sobered.

"Then the *padre* came and offered
Prayers for me . . . and all the yearning
And desire for liquor left me
When the Master smiled and nodded."

Disbelief appeared on faces
Of the silent, awed onlookers.

X

Then the *padre* smiled upon them:
"Many miracles have happened
In this holy sanctuary . . .
Countless times the blessed Savior
Has released the shabby burdens
Of his children at this table.

"When you gaze upon the sacred
Reredos behind the altar
With the hallowed, consecrated
Paintings, you can feel His presence.
He is very near His children
And will answer supplications
Freely if one will but make them

In sincerity. The humble
Heart can always count upon Him.
Edwin sought His consolation
In a spirit of contrition
And He gave it to him gladly."

XI

As the *padre* finished speaking
Spiritual communion gripped the
Little band of humbled humans . . .

"Shall we pray?" the *padre* questioned.
Overawed, Kit Carson stammered,
"Help my unbelief, O Master."

"Make me strong . . . and give me courage
To be faithful to Thy people,"
Bent's words came unbidden from him.

Bridger crossed himself and said, "Lord,
Thank Thee for this precious moment.
Let me take it ever with me
To remember and to cherish—
One glad moment with my Savior . . . "

Lone Coyote's eyes looked upward:
"Would, Great Spirit, that the tattered
Remnants of Thy red-skinned children
Could be knit again together
That they might stand and be counted
In the ranks of favored people
As they were in days long vanished."

Newton's prayer, low and fervent:

"Father, thank Thee for the countless
Blessings Thou hast given to me—
Would that I were worthy of them!"

David, stretching arms to heaven,
Pled for freedom for his people.

"Mercy on Your wayward offspring,"
Prayed the *padre*. "Give them vision
To adhere to Thy commandment:
'Love thy neighbor as thou lovest
Self' . . . and all men are thy neighbors."

Turning Taosward, Givens uttered
"We have learned a priceless lesson."

XII

Late that night, while others slumbered,
Kit told Newton of the founding
Of the town in Taos Valley:

"San Geronimo de Taos,
Founded well before the Pilgrims
Left their homes in distant England,
Was constructed like a fortress—
All the houses faced a plaza.
Backs of buildings formed a running
Wall that closed into full circle.
Four points on the wall were towered:
Sentries watched in all directions
For the Navajos, Apaches,
Utes, and other redskin raiders.

"Neighbor Indians, the Pueblos,

Furnished water to the settlers
In exchange for common defense
Against warring red marauders.

"During Pope's fierce rebellion
Which occurred in Sixteen Eighty,
Taos residents were driven,
As were all the other Spaniards,
From New Mexico. The village
Was rebuilt some twelve years later
When Don Diego de Vargas
Led his forces in reconquest
Of the storied Indian country.

"The next century was laden
With the rich rewards of progress.
Taos became a far-famed haven
Of the best in Spanish culture.
Rapid growth of agriculture,
Industry and trade relations
Formed an economic pattern
That resulted in good living
Both for Spaniards and the Indians.

"Foremost industry of Taos
Was, and is, the huge distillery
Where the great supply of surplus
Grain is utilized in making
Fiery liquor — 'Taos Lightning,'
Used by mountain men in trading
With the Indians. The 'fire water'
Is transported to far reaches
Of Expansive Indian country
On pack mules by traders-trappers.

"No fiesta, dance or party
In the region is in top style
Without plenty of Taos Lightning.

"The distillery was leader
Of industrial advancement
West of Mississippi River.

XIII

"Reputation of the village
As a center of refinement
Spread across the entire country.
Missions, churches, monasteries,
Sturdy homes and business houses
Were established in the valley.

"By mid Seventeen and Fifty
Caravans from Chihuahua
Were arriving and the Taos Trade Fairs
Made of Taos a booming mecca
Where the colonists and Indians,
French fur trappers and the Mountain
Men, American fur traders,
Met to barter and make merry.

"When the earnings of the trappers
Were exhausted, they replenished
Their supplies and journeyed outward
To the wild and virgin mountains
Where their livelihood existed.

XIV

" . . . It has changed but little since then.
We still have our fine relations

With the traders and the Indians,
Though the red men have grown restless
Since construction of the Marcy
Fort in Santa Fe and other
Indications of the coming
Occupation by Americans.
It is possible that trouble
Lies not too far in the offing.
Be that as it may, we're happy.

"Here the past is always present,
And the future holds great promise.
I enjoy the multi-featured
Life I lead in this great country:
Hunting, trapping, scouting, ranching,
All are quite remunerative—
Not so much, perhaps, in money
As in sense of contribution
To advancement of the region.

"If you plan to leave tomorrow,
As you said, it's my suggestion
That we get some rest. Our breakfast
Will be served at early daybreak."

XV

. . . Some three miles beyond the northern
Limit of the valley hamlet
Newton and the others entered
The impressive ancient townsite
Of the Taos Pueblo Indians.
Two five-story massive structures
Housed the thrifty farmers-hunters.

165

Built of durable adobe,
Outside walls were three to seven
Feet in thickness, made to withstand
Onslaught of whatever nature.

Rising stories of the structures
Each receded by the depth of
One room. Entrances to dwellings
Were through roofs by means of ladders
That could be withdrawn, affording
Great security for dwellers.

Through the center of the village
Flowed a rushing crystal river
Which provided ample water
For the irrigation systems
Used to grow abundant crops of
Melons, corn, and beans and squashes.

Rugged mountains in the background
Furnished deer and elk and turkeys
Which completed balanced diets
For the ancient valley dwellers.

Newton watched in fascination
As the women did their baking
In adobe outdoor ovens.

The Pueblo had not changed since
Hernando de Alvarado
Paid a visit to the Indians
Earlier by some three hundred
Years, when Coronado's army
Made its journey through the country.
Alvarado said the Indians

Had a high degree of culture,
And a well-developed system
Of democracy was practiced.

Standing in the northeast corner
Of the hamlet was a mission
Built in Sixteen Ten-Eleven
Under careful supervision
Of a kind Franciscan *padre*
Named Zamora. Sacred paintings,
Images of Christ and Mary,
Rare adornments, native carvings
Graced the holy hand-hewn altar.
Newton musingly repeated:

"Go ye into all the world and
Preach the gospel to all people."
Then he bowed his head, petitioned
Christopher to speed his journey
Homeward to his love, Lucinda.

Without incident they traveled
Back to Towson Fort by way of
The enchanted Clear Fork Valley . . .
Newton waxed enthusiastic
As he pointed out to Edwin
The advantages and beauty
Of the spot he had selected
For his dream home with Lucinda:

"I shall build a timeless token
Of the west. Its grandeur, bigness
Shall be symbolized in limestone—
Like our love 'twill last forever."

167

"Such ambition is inspiring,"
Edwin said. "May I assist you?
I might partially repay you
For the things you've done to help me."

"Thank you. I accept," said Newton.
"I shall buy a good foundation
Herd of cattle. You can run them
At Fort Towson till we're ready
To move to the Clear Fork Valley.
I will also buy a small flock
Of sheep and some blooded horses—
And I want some hounds for hunting."

"Seems like I'll be busy," Edwin
Said. "I'm sure I'll like that!"

Chapter Sixteen

Fort Gibson

INDIAN FLAREUPS at Fort Gibson
Called for transfer from Fort Towson
Of the Givenses and Marcys.

Social life was very active
At Fort Gibson. Parties, dances,
Get-togethers, fishing, picnics
Were enjoyed between assignments
Of men sent to quell disturbance
On the sprawling reservation.

Shortly they were well acquainted
With the families of soldiers,
Traders, settlers and the leaders
Of the Indian population.

It was while they lived at Gibson
That a daughter came to join them.
If it were a girl, they planned to
Name her Jacqueline in honor
Of Lucinda's Grand-Mere DuPuy.
But when she arrived and Newton
Looked her over, he said simply:

"She's so tiny that the only
Name that fits her is Miss Bitsy."

Said Lucinda, in agreement,
"You are right, her name is Bitsy."

II

" . . . I should like to see Diana,"
Said Lucinda on a Sunday
Afternoon. "I'll get the surrey,"
Newton answered. "Come on, David."

Cherokee Diana Rogers,
A survivor of the Tear Trail,
Was a charming, naive maiden
When Sam Houston wooed and won her.

Twenty years had passed since Houston
Built the house, Wigwam Neosho,
High above the deep blue river
For his shy young bride, Diana.

They were happy in the Wigwam
Until destiny called Houston
To the troubled land of Texas . . .
Fair Diana would not follow.
She refused to leave her people—
"No more Tear Trails, please," she pleaded.

"It is said that on occasion
When the mental strains and stresses
Of high office rise to plague him,
He still comes to see Diana,"
Sighed Lucinda. "How romantic!"

Dressed in black, demure Diana
Welcomed Newton and Lucinda.
Lemonade and sugar cookies
Were enjoyed as they chatted.

Snowy curtains fluttered gently
As a breeze blew in the window.
Furniture of burnished walnut
Was arranged in tasteful manner.
Marble tops on large stand tables
Glistened, bearing testimony
To Diana's good housekeeping.

At Diana's firm insistence,
They agreed to stay for supper.
It was getting dark and Newton
Lit the lamp and brought in stove wood.

On the mantel, made of native
Stone, reposed a family Bible
And a dozen little trophies
Saved and treasured by Diana—
Gifts presented by Sam Houston.
The puncheon floor, with hand-woven
Rug, was white around the edges—
The result of many scrubbings.

Shadows crept from every corner
In defiance of the polished
Hurricane lamp with its puny
Bat-shaped flame that fumed and fluttered.

Newton and Lucinda listened
To the ticking of the tall clock—
It was friendly, like Diana . . .

171

And they could not help but wonder
At the tales that it might tell them
If the ticking turned to talking.

III

. . . At a little get-together
In the Marcy home one evening,
Conversation drifted into
Mysticism of the Indians . . .

Several anecdotes were bandied
Back and forth between the menfolk
Till a deeper note was sounded,
And the conversation centered
On the beautiful, intriguing
Aspects of the timely subject.

Randolph, noting Newton's silence
And his strange preoccupation,
Quipped: "A penny for your thoughts, Newt!"

"I was thinking, Randolph . . . thinking
Of a scene that I have harbored
In my memory for weeks now.
Somehow, it has seemed too unreal
To relate, but it surpasses
Anything I've heard this evening
On the fascinating subject
That has been under discussion."

"Ah," Lucinda smiled, "my husband
Has been keeping secrets from me!"

"Come now, Newton," Mary chided,
"You are with friends. Tell your story!"

'Yes," the others chorused, "tell us!"

Newton said, "You won't believe it . . .
Sometimes I myself imagine
That I never really witnessed
The events of which I tell you.

IV

"Some time back, while on a mission
Up the Washita, I wandered
Into an enchanted canyon,
Sacred to the race of red men.
Lone Coyote introduced me
To an Indian priestess-scholar.

"Dressed in soft and snowy doeskin,
Graced with rare artistic beadwork,
She was goddess-like in bearing . . .

"Porcupine quills worked in mystic
Patterns on her gleaming feathered
Jacket symbolized her status.

"Young and beautiful and filled with
Time's accumulated lore of
Civilized tribes, she related:

" 'Maiden-priestess of my tribesmen,
Mother-to-daughter succession
Of a hundred generations,
I should find delight in telling
You the highlights of my people.'

"Please proceed," I promptly told her.
"You will find my ear receptive."

V

" 'Nations' social culture prior
To the advent of the white man,
Was for ages permeated
With an honor that was ever
Placed upon the highest altar.
Tribal laws were few. Agnostics
Were unknown and the Great Spirit
Ruled, for many Nation members
Were enthusiastic mystics—
Devotees of occultism.
They could see the hand eternal
In the universal beauty
Of the earth and in the glory
Of the distant starry heavens.
Animals and birds and fishes,
Flowers and trees and tranquil waters
Sang their songs of the Great Spirit.
Through the wind and rain and thunder,
Through the silence of the summit,
They communed with the Great Spirit . . .
Their devotion makes one wonder:
How superior are white men?

VI

" 'After question of removal
Of the Nations to the west lands
Entered politics, and Jackson,
Who had previously engaged in
Warfare with us, was elected
President, the strong resistance

174

To removal terminated.

" 'Andrew Jackson's overruling
Of Supreme Court and Great Spirit
Took away the hapless Nations'
Sacred heritage and birthright.

" 'In the exodus of nations
Through a wilderness of sorrow,
Hardship, illness and starvation
Stalked us . . . hundreds died . . . and many
Became shattered hulks . . . unable
To regain their health when journeys
Ended in the Territory.

" 'Speckled Snake, the great Creek chieftain,
Speaking to the National Council
Of the Creeks, in the mid-thirties,
Said with disillusioned frankness:
'Brothers, Great White Father tells us
That he loves his Indian children . . .
When the white man came to our shores,
Red men gave him land and kindled
Fires to warm him and to comfort.
When the Spaniards came from south lands
And would have his scalp, our young men
Drew their tomahawks to help him,
And the Spaniards soon were vanquished.

" 'When the white man had warmed himself
At the Indian's fire and eaten
Indian hominy, he became
Large indeed — our Great White Father!
One fork of his tongue declares that

He possesses love for red men,
While the other fork is saying:
Move a little farther westward
Lest by accident I hurt you . . .
With one foot he kicks us westward
While the other rudely tramples
On the graves of our dead fathers . . .
Every time that he expresses
His affection, he continues:
Move a little farther westward—
'Tis a country green and pleasant,
And it shall be yours forever,
As long as grass shall grow and rivers
Run . . . ' says loving Great White Father.

" 'Brothers, I have listened many
Times to talks by our White Father,
Always they begin and end with—
And we always may expect it—
Move a little farther westward.'

VII

" 'Now the past is gone and forsooth
We know but the puny present
Which is like a fragile flower
Born to bloom for one fleet moment
Then to die . . . A sad illusion?
Or will it be back tomorrow?
Yesterday, mayhap, it also
Bloomed atop some distant mountain!
Verily, it springs eternal!

" 'Is there then a past and future?
Are they cryptic endless eons
Bound together by the present?
Surely there could be no present
Had there been no past. The future
Could be simply a delusion—
Certainly, no one has been there!
Gone the past . . . Unknown the future.
Let the flower of the present
Be your glory, spur your journey
Toward the heights of great achievement.
Let its fragrance and its beauty
Span them both . . . and last forever!

" 'In event there is a future,
Let us gaze upon its pages:
On the scroll of time emblazoned
I see names of many red men
Living in the Territory:
The Oowaties, Rosses, Ridges,
Boudinots, Leflores, and Colberts;
Billy Bowlegs and Yahola,
Houston, an adopted tribesman,
William McIntosh, John Jolly,
Little Carpenter, McGilivray,
Allen Wright and Jesse Chisholm,
Drowning Bear and Dragging Canoe,
Pushmataha and Sequoyah
Are a few whose names are deathless
In the annals of the Nations.

" 'In this galaxy of nobles
Are professional men and tradesmen;

Orators and educators,
Military men and statesmen.
Lawyers, doctors, writers, churchmen.

" 'Members of the Civilized Tribes
Are as proud as any people
Of their heritage and culture—
This despite the fact that white men,
Since the time of their arrival,
Have abused and persecuted,
Cheated, robbed, demoralized them.

" 'I have spoken. Lone Coyote,
I am sure your friend is worthy
Or you never would have brought him
Here to see me, but I ask you
Not to bring another white man,
Ever, to Enchanted Canyon'."

. . . All those present complimented
Newton on the able manner
In which he had told his story.
And they noticed he was shaken
As he said goodnight and whispered:
"Come, Lucinda, we must go now.
It grows late. I know you're weary."

As they walked back to their quarters,
Newton felt Lucinda's question,
And he answered slowly, firmly:
"Yes . . . dear heart . . . it really happened."

After a year at Fort Gibson,
They were transferred back to Towson.

Chapter Seventeen

Gold Rush

EIGHTEEN FORTY-NINE dawned brightly.
Talk of gold and fascinating
California adventure
Broke monotony of lonely
Outposts. Fort Smith legislators
Were petitioned to bring pressure
On the congress of the nation
For a military highway
From Fort Smith to California.

Fort Smith at the time was teeming
With a horde of Forty-Niners
Anxious to begin the journey
Through the vast unknown, far-stretching,
To the California gold fields.

Randolph Marcy was instructed
To escort the Forty-Niners
To Santa Fe via northern
Roads and to return by southern
Trails in order to establish
Safest routes of western travel.

Marcy, having heard from Newton
Of his travels in the country,

Asked if he would not accompany
Him, and Newton said Lucinda
Planned to visit Crescent City;
Consequently, he would welcome
Opportunity to join him.

In early spring the procession
Left Fort Smith through Territory
Of the Indians. Early stages
Of the journey were a festive
Time for travelers. They enjoyed it.

Cheerfully and with gay banter
They approached the barren stretches
Of America's "Zahara"—
Land of waste and desolation,
Irreclaimable, eternal.
Here the banter turned to fearful
Cursing of the untoward hardships
That beset unseasoned travelers.

Wearily they toiled toward frugal
Water holes that dotted treeless
Badlands basking in the silence
Of the sunbaked earth and cacti.

Screeching wheels and clanking harness
Were new sounds to Staked Plains country
Where the stillness had been broken
Only by resounding rumble
Of the buffalo and cayuse,
Scream of panther, howl of lobo.

Single file across the desert
Snaked the caravan of wagons

Drawn by horses, mules and oxen.
Extra livestock—horses, cattle—
Followed the train slowly wending
Ever westward toward the gold fields:
Hardy, reckless Forty-Niners
Blazing trails to the Pacific
For America to follow.

II

Santa Fe was reached the latter
Part of June, eight hundred twenty
Miles and eighty-five days after
Leaving Fort Smith. Soon the return
Journey, via Dona Ana,
Onward through the Clear Fork Valley,
Started. When they reached the ranch site,
Givens pointed out to Marcy
All advantages provided
By the lavish hand of nature—
Stone for building, water, pastures—
For an ideally located
Ranch. Said Marcy, "It is perfect.
You should have your sheep and cattle
Out here now. This is the finest
Grass I've seen in all the country.
Certainly, there is no limit
As to the number of cattle
One could raise in Clear Fork Valley.
By the way, how are your livestock?"

"They are fine," responded Givens.
"When we left, there were six hundred
Cows and probably that many

Sheep and forty-six good horses.
And, Randolph, I am proud of Edwin.
He is now a first rate stockman—
And with dogs he is a master.

"He's a good man," Marcy answered.
"I recall the day I met him—
When he was a wild-eyed drunkard,
Incoherent, forlorn, wasted.
His deliverance was a godsend."

"Aye, a miracle," said Newton.

Winter hung upon the landscape
When the eighteen covered wagons
Rolled at high noon into Towson.

By coincidence, Lucinda
Had returned three days ahead of
Newton. Their reunion was a
Second honeymoon of blissful
Days that stretched to bursting springtime.

III

On a spring day, Randolph Marcy
Said, "I'm told the fish are biting!
Could we not arrange a camping
Trip? Just yesterday 'Miz' Mary
Said she would enjoy an outing."

"That is not a bad idea,"
Answered Newton, "I would wager
That I might create some interest
In that area. Lucinda
Well could use some relaxation."

When arrangements were completed,
The two families were joined by
Captain Mayfield and his daughter,
Gwendolyn, and Colonel Lovelace,
Edwin, Captain Sands, and David.

One of the big army wagons,
With an extra set of sideboards,
Carried tents, supplies, and cooking
Utensils and quilts for pallets.
David drove the prancing stallions.
Naught would do the older children
But that they accompany David.
Beauty and the other saddle
Horses trailed behind the wagon.

Specially arranged, the other
Long vehicle had a cross seat
For the driver; Passengers were
Seated on two long spring benches
So that they faced one another.

The place Randolph had selected
For the camp was up Red River,
Fifteen miles beyond Fort Towson.
At noon they stopped for a picnic,
After which the younger children
Napped a while before the journey
Was continued up the valley.

IV

Some three miles from destination
They approached a great plantation.
"It's as beautiful," Lucinda

Said, "as those in Mississippi
Or in our own Louisiana."

"It's magnificent," said Mary.
Gwendolyn exclaimed, "The landscape
Is the prettiest I ever
Saw. The mansion is exquisite!
Tell us all about it, Randolph!"

Randolph laughed at her exuberance:
"On our way home we will visit
The plantation. We'll be welcome
As the owner is a special
Friend of mine. I have a standing
Invitation to sojourn there.

"That is Rose Hill, stately mansion
Of Colonel Robert Jones. His story
Sounds almost like that of Midas.
Colonel is a half-blood Choctaw.
He was born in Mississippi,
Eighteen Eight; was educated
In Kentucky at a tribal
School maintained by Choctaw Nation.

"After exile, he accepted
Work with Berthelet, the trader.
Ere long he became a partner
In a trading post at Doaksville.
From the very start he prospered.
Soon he bought his first plantation—
This three-hundred-acre frontage
On the river. His initial
Yield of cotton was fantastic.

184

"In a few short years his holdings
Have grown into six plantations;
He has rapidly expanded
Into other enterprises,
Including a mill and sugar
Plantation in Louisiana.

"With two partners, he is owner
Of the steamboats *Woodsman, Choctaw,*
Built to his design. They ply the
Arkansaw to Scully Landing
When the Great Raft hampers shipment
Of his cotton down Red River.

"One of the largest slaveholders
In America, he lives a
Life of truly Southern grandeur.

V

"His second wife, Susan Colbert,
Is the talented and pretty
Daughter of Chickasaw half-bloods.
As a wedding gift, he built her,
On his huge Lake West plantation,
Which includes five thousand acres,
An imposing twelve room mansion.
It developed that the humid
Summer weather was a hazard
To the health of his young helpmeet.
As a consequence, the mansion
Is used only during winter.

"Jones immediately started
The construction of this summer

Residence you see before you.
It is a majestic castle.
Louis Fifteenth architecture
Is reflected in its styling.
The interior is finished
In mahogany and walnut,
Oak and maple. Furnishing are
All imported from the finest
Marts in Europe. The refinements
Cannot be excelled in any
Of the country's better mansions.

"As Miss Gwendolyn has told you,"
Marcy winked at Colonel Lovelace,
"Elegance is expressed in
The landscaping. Formal gardens
Blend into orchards and vineyards
In a most delightful manner."

VI

Campground was a sand and gravel
Beach along a cove, deep hidden
In a virgin growth of woodland
Dressed in all the lavish colors
That bespeak the best of springtime.

Fish were plentiful, and Captains
Sands and Mayfield, Colonel Lovelace,
All of whom were able Nimrods,
Soon accounted for abundant
Fresh meat, venison and turkeys,
Buffalo, and elk and pheasants.

Edwin, David and the children,
Walking near camp, found a bee tree
That provided tasty honey.
On the fourth day of the camp-out,
Sometime after noon siesta,
As the children played and waded
In the shallow, lapping water,
David hurried toward the woodland.

"Wonder where he's going?" Edwin
Ventured. "He spent all the morning
In the woods. At noon I noticed
He ate like a half-starved Indian."

VII

"Hark!" said Newton, "I hear bloodhounds."

From the distance came the deep-mouthed
Baying of excited bloodhounds
Hot upon the trail of fleeing
Darkies who could sense the ending
Of a few brief hours of freedom.

Louder grew the mournful baying.
Straight for camp came barking bloodhounds.
Mary and Lucinda gathered
Up the children; Newton placed them
In a wagon, turned and followed
Colonel Lovelace and the others
Who were hurriedly descending
On a spot not fifty yards from
Camp site where the sniffing bloodhounds
Paused perplexed and in confusion.
Close behind the hounds came riders,

187

Cursing, angered by the trouble
The escaping slaves were causing.

"Catch them niggers!" yelled a horseman,
"Hit the trail, you ornery rascals!"

"Hold on, Thomas" said another,
"Those dogs haven't lost a quarry
Since I've owned 'em; something's wrong here."

Suddenly the earth was parted
And two badly frightened Negroes
Stood straight up, their arms extended
In a gesture of surrender.

"Nigger lovers!" spat the owner
Of the dogs. "Hold on a minute,"
Snapped the colonel. "I assure you
We are innocent of any
Part in this, and your abusive
Words will not be tolerated."

Randolph, Newton quickly sided
Colonel Lovelace. Edwin, Captains
Sands and Mayfield hurried over
To the Negroes to protect them
From the lashes of the horsewhip
Carried by the irate owner.

"They were cleverly concealed, sir,"
Said the young plantation foreman
To the colonel in an effort
To pour oil on troubled waters.
"My friends jumped to the conclusion
That you helped them. We believe you

When you say you had no knowledge
Of the hide-out. We are sorry
And apologize for bursts of
Temper." "Very well," said Lovelace.

When the party had departed,
Newton smiled and called out: "David!"

"I'se up heah, Suh, Mistah Newton,"
David said and started climbing
From his perch in a tall oak tree.

Back at camp the conversation
Centered on the clever manner
In which David had concealed the
Slaves in his attempt to aid them.

VIII

"Colonel, Lovelace," teen-age Tommy
Asked, "would you explain how slavery
Started? I don't understand it."

"Neither do I," said the colonel.
"It's a tough and knotty problem:
Biblical accounts relate that
Babylonians, Chaldeans,
Hebrews, Romans, Greeks, Egyptians,
All subscribed to human bondage.
History of other nations
Reveals that some form of bondage
Has been recognized by most men.

"Negro slavery is ancient,
And the big boom in the market,
Which came in the eighteenth century,

Put a virtual end to traffic
In enslavement of white people.

"Drudgery involved in raising
Cotton and tobacco called for
Importation of slave labor,
And the African slave market
Was developed to supply it.

"Slowly, though, the tide is turning,
And the day will come when freedom
Is restored to those in bondage.

"Abolitionists are urging
Gradual emancipation
Of the slaves with compensation
To their masters. Liberation
Has already come for many.

"A small town of liberated
Bondsmen at Cape Mesurcado,
Africa, is slowly growing.
In Eighteen Seven, legislation
Was enacted that prohibits
Importation of additional
Slaves into the States United.
The law is loosely enforced and
Smuggling is an active business.
Most of the slaves coming into
America today are from
The West Indies, not Africa.

"It is obvious that the two
We saw captured in the woods are
Contraband. They spoke no English,

And the man who owned them stated
They were very amateurish
In performance of their labor.
Second, third, fourth-generation
Slaves perform their many duties
Well. They fit into a pattern
That affords them some enjoyment
From the life we force upon them.
Many of them are devoted
To their masters. Still the moral
Issue should be clear to free men:
All, regardless of their color,
Are a part of God's creation;
And, in His sight, please be certain
There is not the least distinction.

"Lavish profits of slave running
Induce many men to enter
The illicit trade and countless
Blacks are brought into this region.

"Usually the trade is practiced
In collusion with enforcers
Of the law — a U. S. Marshal
Or his deputies — those willing
To accept the tainted money.
From the gulf coast slaves are smuggled
Up the Sabine and Red rivers
To a ready, eager market.
When a sale is made, the smuggler
Takes his gold and hastens back to

The West Indies for another
Load of forlorn, luckless Negroes.

"When the charges are delivered,
An informer tells the marshal,
Waiting at a designated
Place, and he goes into action:
U. S. Marshals are empowered
To confiscate the illegal
Entrants and to dispose of them
At a so-called public auction.
"One-half of the price of purchase
Is the marshal's, and the balance
Is awarded the informer.
Inasmuch as the real owner
Is the one and only bidder,
The price is low. All are happy:
All, that is, except the chattel.
Then the marshal gives a legal
Bill of sale which is conclusive
Evidence of lawful entry
Of the slave into this country."

"Gee," said Tommy, "what an awful
Way for men to treat each other."

"I agree," said Colonel Lovelace,
And the others nodded assent.

Chapter Eighteen

Journey to Fredericksburg

EIGHTEEN FIFTY, February,
Orders came for Newton Givens
And eight other Towson soldiers
To report forthwith for duty
On the far frontier of Texas.

Fredericksburg, a German village,
Was, like other frontier hamlets,
Suffering from raids by Indians.

Strong petitions of frontiersmen,
Urgent treaty obligations,
And the desire to encourage
More expansion to the westward
Had influenced fast construction
Of a string of military
Posts across the Texas outlands.

Martin Scott, first fort established
In the new string, was located
Two miles from the struggling German
Hamlet in Comanche country.

Newton, on receipt of orders,
Said, "Lucinda, please consider
Going to New Orleans until
I can look the country over
And be certain you will like it."

"No alternative is given
You . . . You have to follow orders,"
Said Lucinda. "Since you offer
Me a choice, I choose to follow
You, my dear. My heart commands me!"

"Spoken like the cherished helpmeet
That you are, my sweet Lucinda!
I knew better than to ask you . . .
Still, it is a land of hardship,
And I hesitate to take you—
It may be rough on the children."

"Do not speak to me of hardship,"
Smiled Lucinda as she kissed him.
"There is no such thing in heaven,
And, where you are, is my Eden."

II

Monday morning, wagons loaded,
And the big mules lined in tandem,
The small party left for Preston,
First stop in the state of Texas.

In an ambulance ahead of
Three lumbering army wagons,
Newton and Lucinda chatted.
"I have never been to Preston,"

Said Lucinda. "You and others
Have referred to it quite often.
I am under the impression
That it is a wicked village.
Now that we are going through it,
I should like details about it."

"Your impression is correct, dear.
I stopped there while on a mission
Last month; and a friend, Dan Tilden,
Brought me up to date on Preston.

"With the California gold fields
Calling, immigrants by thousands
Stop in Preston for provisions
And a last spree before jumping
Off into the boundless unknown.

"Reckless spending by the splurgers
Has produced a border boom town,
Drawing riffraff like a magnet.
Preston is the wildest sin town
Spawned since Sodom and Gomorrah.
The very air is polluted
With the stench of bawdy houses,
Gun smoke, scum, and rot-gut whiskey.

"Crime is rampant. Lurid murders
Go unsolved, and decent people
Double-bar their doors at sunset.
Salted with intrigue, corruption,
All the filth of human offal
Seems to find its way to Preston.
Renegades and desperadoes,

Outlaws, harlots, gamblers, killers,
Black sheep, lost sheep, thieves, and robbers
Ply their trades in wild abandon.
Law is unknown and the outcasts
Live a heartbeat from perdition.

"Small town innocents and farm boys,
Free for first time from protective
Guidance of their watchful elders,
Are plucked clean of cash and virtue.
Some are drugged and rolled for money;
They are fortunate, as others
Are killed outright for possessions—
Boot Hill does a thriving business.

"Self-respecting, honest townsmen
Can only pray that the orgy
Of depravity and sodden
Immorality will perish
In its self-created maelstrom
Of debauchery and evil."

"Certainly it sounds revolting,"
Said Lucinda. "If we have to
Spend the night there, what will we do?"
"We'll be welcome at the Tildens,"
Newton answered. "But my plans are
To pass through the town in daytime.
You may rest assured, however,
That the army is respected,
Even in the town of Preston."

III

. . . As they traveled toward the Torrey
Trading posts, the warming sunshine

Poured down brightly, as the Texas
Winter that year was a mild one.
Every sound and view was cheerful.
Every prospect was most pleasing.
Little Newton prattled gayly,
And the baby laughed as Newton
Kissed her neck and stole her sugar.

Canvas sides of the ambulance
Were rolled high to let the sunshine
Add its pleasure to the journey.
Old blue uniforms and sassy
Mules and ever-changing landscapes
Pleased the eye. The heavy grating
Of the brakes, the cheerful swearing
Of the drivers were like music
To the ears of those who heard them.
The trip was hard, but interesting.

Each morn as the soldiers bundled
Her tent, ashes held Lucinda's
Gaze . . . "The ashes are the remains,"
Mused Lucinda as they smouldered,
"Of my home for a few moments
In the journey of a lifetime.
I am lonely as I leave them,
And they have a poignant meaning.
. . . Walls and beams are necessary
Parts of houses, but a home is
Built of love and dreams and stardust—
It can be along a barren
Trail that stretches far through Texas.
So strong is the loving instinct

197

Of home in my inner being
That the tiny, twining tendrils
Shoot out in a single nighttime
To enmesh me. There is subt'e
Fascination and high moments
Of contentment at the camp sites
I have known on Texas prairies."

IV

In hill country, where the roadway
Wound into a narrow canyon,
An alarmed, bedraggled white man
Slipped from hiding to accost them.
Fearfully he told of horror
Visited upon his party:
A three-wagon immigrant train
Had been waylaid by Comanches.

Other members of the party—
Two men with their wives and children—
Had been ambushed: covered wagons
Were destroyed and their possessions
Stolen by the red marauders.

The onslaught had come at twilight
Of the day before. The camp site
Had been poorly situated
And was easy prey for raiders.

As they neared the camp, the soldiers,
Acting under Newton's orders,
Rode ahead with the still frightened,
Half-crazed immigrant, Jim Jordan,

Who had fled the bloody foray.
Charred remains of the burned wagons
And the mutilated bodies
Of the victims told a story
Oft repeated on the frontier.

All the party was accounted
For excepting two teen-agers,
Daughters of the murder victims,
Taken into slavery by the
Indians — truly death were better.

After burying the bodies,
Givens called his men to council.
Jordan thought that the Comanches
Might be waiting in recesses
Of the passage from the canyon.

There was no course for the wagons
Except straight ahead. Said Newton:
"Check your guns and ammunition.
Be prepared for instant trouble.
Lead off, Hogan, we will follow."

V

Then his voice assumed a soothing
Tone that belied his foreboding.
"Listen closely, my Lucinda:
I am sure there are no Indians
In the pass, so be not fearful.
But in case I am mistaken,
There's a chance they might attack us.
If they do, and I am wounded,

199

Or if it appears full certain
They will take us, there is only
One thing to be done — so do it . . . "

Placing derringers beside her,
Newton whispered, "Do not let them
Take you, darling, or the children."

Lying quietly on blankets
On the floor of the ambulance
With the youngsters close beside her,
Lucinda's thoughts flashed to other
Years. In swift review came visions
Of New Orleans and her mother . . .
Of Annette, Nanette, and Edwin;
Of The Oaks and Grand-Mere DuPuy . . .
Of excursions, parties, dances,
And a summer spent in Europe . . .
Then the golden years with Newton
Passed in panoramic splendor—
"God," she prayed, "let them continue;
Still, if this must be the ending,
Thank you, Lord, for sending Newton
My way . . . God, the bit of heaven
That he brought me is ecstatic—
Do not let it turn to ashes . . ."
Then her eyes looked up and fastened
On her husband's grim-set features.
His gaze wandered over every
Inch of earth on the left side of
The ambulance; on the right side
Rode a dragoon with his carbine
Poised for instant, deadly action.

Journey to Fredericksburg

As the wagons rattled onward,
Not a single word was spoken.
Each tense moment seemed to lengthen
Into hours as sleek mules plodded
Steadily along the rough trail.

Derringers in hands, Lucinda
Gazed upon her helpless babies.
She was wondering if her courage
Was sufficient for her orders.

Finally the country opened
To a far and peaceful vista—
Indians had long since departed.

Memories of throbbing blue-veined
Temples hedged by Titian ringlets,
And of derringers held ready,
Seared Lucinda's inmost being.

VI

One week later their arrival
At Fort Scott was celebrated
By a rousing frontier welcome.
Life at Fort Scott was exciting.
Soldiers constantly patrolling
Indian country, told of many
Thrilling bouts with young Comanches
Who delighted in harrassing
Settlers and attacking travelers.
Often when Lucinda finished
Household duties, she would visit
Homesteads near the sturdy fortress.

Many friendships were established
With the gentle, well-bred *hausfraus*.

When the harvest moon hung brightly
In the heavens, Fredericksburgers
Planned a ball *der Verheiraten*.*
They invited Fort Scott soldiers
And their ladies. *Vereins Kirche*,
Combination fort, church, school, and
Social center was a-glitter
With the light of lamps and candles.
Couples swung in graceful rhythm
As they danced the pretty German
Dances in their Old World brilliance.

Newton and Lucinda, resting
From a couple hours of dancing,
Chatted with the Kannenbergers.
"Won't you tell me," asked Lucinda,
"Why you charming, cultured people
Left the gracious courts of Europe
For the wilds of frontier Texas
Where you live with constant danger?"

VII

"It's a long and tragic story,"
Heinrich Kannenberger answered.
"Let me start at the beginning:
Eighteen Forty-four, in autumn,
German Prince Carl zu Selms-Braunfels,
Heading *Adelsverein*, royal

* A dance for married couples

Order of German immigrants,
Met the first of new arrivals
At Galveston. We were taken
By small craft to Carlshafen,
Where we spent our first bleak Christmas
In the alien land of Texas.
Previous to our arrival
A large land grant had been purchased
Some three hundred miles northwestward.

"Early Forty-five, initiál
Caravans of royal settlers
Headed inland toward the farm lands.
Disappointed and discouraged
By slow progress and great distance,
We encamped at Victoria
While Prince Carl went in search of
Nearer lands that we might settle.

"At San Antonio, Prince Carl
Learned of Comal Springs where water
Was available and fertile
Acres stretched in all directions.
Captivated by its beauty,
Prince Carl purchased two leagues of it.
New Braunfels, the name selected,
Honored Prince Carl's great ancestral
Domain in the mother country.

"Months that followed were a torment:
Several thousand Germans landed
At the port of Carlshafen.
But there was no transportation
To be had to move them inland.

War with Mexico commanded
The attention of all teamsters.

"Many tried to make the journey
On foot. Countless numbers perished.
The trail from the coast was lined with
Graves of immigrants who sickened
And died en route to New Braunfels.

"Next, financial difficulties
And disease beset the hamlet—
Hard we battled for existence.

"When Prince Carl returned to Europe,
Management of the colony
Fell to energetic Baron
Von Muesbach. The situation
Bettered under his direction.
To make room for steady streams of
Settlers, Meusbach purchased new lands
Farther inland, sent surveyors
To establish a good roadway
To the newly-purchased land grant.

"Eighteen Forty-six, late springtime,
We moved inland from New Braunfels
To the Pedernales Valley,
In this verdant, lush hill country.
Fredericksburg, the name chosen
For the new and hopeful townsite,
Honored Frederick the Great of
Prussia, who himself was member
Of *Adelsverein*, and patron.
During its first year the hamlet

Lost, through cholera epidemics,
Scores of people, and the Indians
Took the lives of many others.
At night all streets were deserted
As precaution against red men.

"Able diplomat, John Meusbach—
Long since he had dropped his title—
Called Comanche chiefs together
And negotiated treaties.
The Comanches, through their chieftains,
Old Owl, Santanna, and others
Have a keen respect for Meusbach,
Who, because of his flowing red beard,
They call *El Sol Colorado.**

"Small bands of young braves, hot-headed,
Still burn homes and steal our horses,
Scalp our travelers, and wreak havoc
In a dozen ways, but credit,
As a tribe, is due Comanches
For their great respect for treaties
We negotiated with them.

" . . . Stuffy pomp and ceremony
Of the drawing rooms of Europe
Are forgotten in our exchange
For new freedom of the prairies
And the rolling hills of Texas.

"We are learning that your buckskin
Is more practical than velvet.
Bowie knives and caps of coon skin
Replace rapiers and courtly

* The Red Sun

Plumes. Our titles are discarded.
We are happily adjusting
To our new life. It surpasses
All of Europe's ostentation."

Kannenberger's story ended
As the dancers were preparing
To retire. Lucinda thanked him
For an entertaining evening.

VIII

Logic does not enter into
An accounting for the whims of
Officialdom of the army:
Six months after the arrival
Of the Givenses at Fort Scott,
Orders came for his transference,
With twelve other Fort Scott soldiers,
Back to Indian Territory.

"Since I'm in command," said Newton,
As the wagon train moved outward,
"This trip you shall see your future
Home site in the Clear Fork Valley."

"Oh, how thrilling," trilled Lucinda,
"Secretly I've rather envied
It because I have not seen it.
Your description of the valley,
And the feeling you have for it,
Somehow almost make me jealous.
When you speak of it, the sparkle
In your eyes resembles star dust."

At Austin wagons veered northwestward
In a beeline for the Clear Fork.
Dusk was kissing the horizon
As the little train of wagons
Moved into the quiet valley.

"Shall we camp here?" asked Private
Callahan, when Newton halted
To take bearings of the country.
"No," said Newton, pointing northward,
"By that high knoll over yonder
Is a spring of living water
And a creek. We'll spend the night there.
It will be dark when we reach it,
But it is ideal for camping.
We will spend tomorrow morning
In the valley. While Lucinda
And I look the country over,
You and others will make repairs
On the wagons, and the horses
And mules can get some extra grazing."

IX

Aromatic tang of wood smoke
Mingled with the tantalizing
Smell of bacon and black coffee
Met Lucinda when she wakened.
The horizon was aflame with
Gorgeous hues of red and orange.
An autumnal air of crispness
Hung across the waking valley
As she gazed upon the scenic
Wonderland outspread before her.

They had camped upon the north bank
Of a crystal brook that wandered
Lazily across the prairie
Toward the Clear Fork of the Brazos;
It was lined with trees of walnut.
Nearby rose a sparkling, bubbling
Spring of clear and cooling water.

Nature had arranged the landscape
So that beauties of the valley
Were displayed from every angle.
Newton, glancing from his coffee,
Saw Lucinda's admiration
Mirrored in her beaming features
As she gazed across the valley.

"Well, my darling," queried Newton,
"How do you like my selection
Of a place to spend a lifetime?"

Solemnly Lucinda answered:
"If you looked the whole world over,
As, in fact, you have my dearest,
You could not have found a better
Spot to homestead. 'Tis the Garden!
It's so picturesque and lovely
That I never want to leave it.
I wish we could move tomorrow.
Now I understand my jealous
Feeling toward the Clear Fork Valley."

After breakfast they proceeded
To inspect the virgin splendors
Of the land they had adopted.

From his mind's eye Newton pictured
For Lucinda plans for building . . .
His description was so vivid
That the ranch took shape before them.

"Oh, I love it," said Lucinda,
Joining in the conversation.
"I should like to name the little
Creek meandering toward the river
'Walnut,' it is so befitting."

"Walnut Creek it is," said Newton.
"Over there," he gestured eastward,
"Since you've seen the place and like it,
I propose to start construction
Of a stock pen just as soon as
I can hire the right stone masons.

"I will get some help for Edwin;
He can move the horses, cattle,
Sheep and hounds into the valley.
We can build the ranch house later."

"That will be a thrill for Edwin,"
Said Lucinda." He was feeling
Crowded when we left Fort Towson."

"Out here he will surely never
Feel the pinch of nearby neighbors.
There is not a single settler
Short of Santa Fe or Bent's Fort,"
Newton said. "Well, let's be going."

Chapter Nineteen

Belknap and Phantom Hill

DOWN THE MARCY Trail in Texas
Givens rode with the command of
Major General William Belknap.
Belknap had been ordered to build
A new cordon of protective
Military installations.

Eighteen Fifty-one the frontier
Was in throes of mounting Indian
Turbulence, unrest, and warfare.
June the thirteenth found the party
On the Red Fork of the Brazos.
June the twenty-fourth saw Belknap
Staking out a fort location
Ten miles down from Marcy's Crossing—
The first post in Northwest Texas.

While the fortress was in process
Of construction, General Belknap
Planned to go with Randolph Marcy,
Newton Givens, and a party
Of explorers and surveyors
On a trip to Pecan Bayou
And the Concho River where two

More forts were to be established.

At this point news of the sudden
Death of General Arbuckle
Came, and Belknap said to Marcy:
"Go ahead and make locations
For the posts and I will journey
To Fort Smith and see that orders
Are not changed for the advancement
Of the Northwest Texas' outlands."

Meanwhile, infant military
Installation suffered hardship.
Drought set in. Sufficient water
Could not be found; consequently,
Belknap moved two miles down river.

. . . Rushing plans for post completion
And establishment of other
Forts the party had located
On the Bayou and the Concho,
General Belknap suffered illness
Of a complicated nature.

II

Changes in the frontier setup
Came in rapid fire succession:
Persifor F. Smith, Commander,
Eighth Military Department,
Unannounced, showed up at Belknap.
He was authorized to alter
Entire plans of border defense.

William Belknap's ailment worsened.
He agreed to make the journey
To Fort Washita hospital,
But he died en route at Preston.

III

Smith, at first, was set on building
Forts at headwaters of Rivers
Concho, Llano, and San Saba,
And a fourth at Caddo Village,
Twenty miles below Fort Belknap.

After due deliberation,
He decided that Fort Belknap
Should remain and that one other
Post would suffice for protection
Of the country for the present.

Casually he glanced at tracings
On his map and drew a circle—
"At this point beside the Clear Fork
We shall build the second fortress,"
He advised his aide . . . and thusly
The location of Fort Phantom
Hill seemed almost accidental.

Of the many streams and rivers
Pulsing lifeblood through the frontier
Few could share the moods and contrasts
Of the long and snaking Brazos
On a fork of which Fort Belknap
Grew in stature and importance.

IV

When Fort Belknap was completed,
Newton hired two good stone masons,
Who had helped to build the fortress,
To construct a combination
Stockpen, storehouse, living quarters
On the Clear Fork Valley ranch site.

It encompassed half an acre,
With a four-foot wide foundation.
Walls were five feet high, convexing
Slightly toward the upper limit.
One of two huge wings was covered
With a shingled roof converting
It into a shed for storage
Of vehicles, harness, saddles,
And some rooms for living quarters.

Edwin, with three men for helpers,
Moved the livestock to the valley.

V

. . . Friday, fourteenth of November,
Eighteen Fifty-one, the westing
Sun gazed down on an approaching
Caravan of army wagons.
Colonel J. J. Abercrombie,
With five companies of soldiers,
Encamped at his destination—
Phantom Hill in Clear Fork Valley.

It was bitter cold. A teamster,
Twenty horses, mules and oxen

213

Died while marching from Fort Belknap,
Last lap of the weary journey
From Fort Washita in Indian
Territory where they started.
Camp was pitched and army rations
Served to travel-weary soldiers.

VI

Early next day, Abercrombie,
In the company of Givens,
Toured immediate surrounding
Country. He was most unhappy
With his findings. Satisfactory
Drinking water, trees for building
Army structures were not present.

Abercrombie's fervent protests
Over building of a fortress
Under such adverse conditions
Went unheeded. Smith had vanished,
For the time, and no official
Change of orders could be managed.
Consequently the construction
Of Fort Phantom moved on schedule.

Some two hundred thirty troopers
Sent to build the fort worked under
A civilian supervisor,
Leonhardt, a master builder.

At the outset work was hampered
By a dearth of proper building
Material. Scrub oak growing

On a sandy ridge just north of
The river and larger timber
Lining banks were quite unsuited
For anything except firewood.

Six miles distant from the post site
Trees for building purposes were
Found, but it was necessary
To haul them in ox-drawn wagons.

Two miles from the fort on east bank
Of Elm Creek a good stone quarry
Was located. Troopers started
The slow process of obtaining
Rocks to be used in erecting
Buildings of substantial nature.

Meanwhile, lean-to's, tents and jacals
Served as shelter from the icy
Blasts of winter. The ingenious
Soldiers chinked the cracks, and cozy
Quarters recompensed their efforts.

It was many weeks before the
Post gained semblance of a fortress.

VII

Water was another drawback.
Personnel and livestock suffered
From drinking unsanitary,
Brackish water of the Clear Fork.
Relief came with the discovery
Of a spring upon a hilltop
Near the fort, but with arrival

Of dry summer months it vanished.
Finally the search for water
Led to digging of a deep well:
Its diameter was twenty
Feet; in depth it reached to eighty.
This well furnished a sufficient
Quantity of drinking water
For a time, but after several
Months of drought it was exhausted.

Water problems reached solution
By assigning a large number
Of ox-wagons, barrel laden,
To the task of hauling water
From a source four miles from Phantom:
Though the water was distasteful,
It was the best yet discovered.

VIII

Soon the nearby firewood sources
Were depleted and another
Dozen wagons were engaged in
Hauling cord wood from receding
Groves of blackjack. Other teamsters
Spent full time hauling provisions
From the distant Austin depot.

Weather likewise added hardships
To already overburdened
Soldiers at the Phantom outpost.
During winter, howling northers
Stung through insufficient clothing.
In the summertime the hot winds

Burned their skins to dark brown color.
During fall and springtime seasons,
They were plagued by searing sandstorms.

Illness was another problem;
Lack of vegetables in diet
And unsatisfactory water
Took the blame for many ailments:
Scurvy, intermittent fever,
Dysentery were quite common.

In the spring, wild plums and onions
Were abundant for a brief time—
Greedily the soldiers ate them.
The post surgeon, Alex Hasson,
Tried in vain to raise a garden.
To improve the dietary
Lack of plant food, Dr. Taylor
Recommended adding pickles
To the daily army ration.
All they did was make men thirsty;
They drank more polluted water
And got sicker; Dr. Taylor
Quickly struck them from the menu.

Abercrombie and some other
Officers brought wives and families
To the post to share a home-life.
On the other hand, enlisted
Men existed in a dreary
World of loneliness and boredom.

IX

Post on Clear Fork of the Brazos
Was official designation

Of the lonely installation,
But throughout the border country
It was always called Fort Phantom.

Primitive and isolated,
It was known as the most forlorn
Station on the entire frontier.
Borderland protection involved
Countless hours of weary marching;
Gnawing pangs of thirst and hunger;
Endless hardships and discomforts.

How the army ever figured
It could conquer the Comanches,
Probably the world's best horsemen,
With the infantry is puzzling.
For that matter, many other
Things the army did at Phantom
Seemed beyond the realm of reason—
Breeding great dissatisfaction
In the breasts of homesick soldiers.

Poor food, clothing, and equipment,
And the lack of recreation,
Were among primary reasons
For the widespread discontentment
That existed at the fortress.

Phantom's entire inventory
Of artillery consisted
Of a pair of antiquated
Cannons — both of them eight-pounders.
Rifles also were out-dated
And of insufficient number
To equip the roll of soldiers:

Musketoons, percussion muskets,
Were the arms the army furnished—
These were rated slightly better
Than the Indians' bows and arrows.

Dislike of the post by troopers
Ripened into sullen hatred;
As a consequence, Fort Phantom
Was bedeviled by desertions.

X

. . . After having helped establish
Fortresses Belknap and Phantom
Givens was assigned to Croghan,
A fort on a tributary
Of the Colorado River
On the borderland dividing
Settlements of pioneering
White men and *Comancheria*.
Days at Croghan were a happy
Time for all the Givens family.

Chapter Twenty

Clear Fork Agency

IN EIGHTEEN Fifty-one, a lawyer,
Jesse Stem, from far Ohio,
Joined the U. S. Indian Service.

Subject to attacks of asthma,
Stem requested an assignment
In the State of Texas, hopeful
That it would prove beneficial
To his health. He went to Fort Graham
For the winter, but in springtime
He established his headquarters
In the Valley of the Clear Fork
At the spreading river crossing
Some halfway between Fort Belknap
And Fort Phantom. His first dwelling
Was a dugout, but with help of
Wards he soon built combination
Picket warehouse-living quarters.

II

Man of tolerance and judgment,
Stem served as confessor-father,

Keeper of the peace, advisor,
And reprover of the red men.
Tact and patience, courage, wisdom,
Were employed in all his dealings
With the Indians of the region.

Leading chieftains of Comanches,
Buffalo Hump and Sanaco,
Pah-hah-yo-ko, and Ketumse
Came to powwow with the agent
And accept his gifts of trinkets,
Blankets, food, beads, and tobacco.

Representatives of other
Indians — Wichitas and Wacos,
Tonkawas, Keechis, and Caddoes—
Called on Stem to seek assistance.
The courageous agent entered
Into tribal controversies
As peacemaker, and his fairness
Won respect, esteem, and honor.

Many times the man enlisted
Help of tribesmen in retrieving
Stolen horses. His influence
Soon was felt throughout the country.

III

Near the agency, the river
Bottom land was rich. Stem plowed it;
Planted corn and oats; his efforts
Were rewarded with a harvest
Far beyond his expectations.
His experimental farming

Disproved claims that insufficient
Rainfall forbade agricultural
Pursuits in the Clear Fork Valley.

Three straight seasons he succeeded
In producing quite abundant
Yields of grain. A ready market
Was nearby. The quartermasters
At Fort Phantom and Fort Belknap
Bought his entire crops; sent wagons
To the agency to haul them
To the installations' storerooms.
Stem's success in agriculture
Helped convince nomadic Indians
That it might be an advantage
To consider sedentary
Living upon lands provided
Through "White Father's" benefaction.

IV

There was turmoil, strife and violence
All along the restless border
As the remnants of once powerful
Eastern Texas tribes, uprooted,
Searched in vain for land to live on.
Several dwindling bands were moving,
Due to pressure of the settlers
And a military crack-down,
North to dreaded reservation
Life in Indian Territory.
The confining reservation
Gave security, in measure,

To the red men. Camp sites, rations
Were provided, but the freedom
To which they were long accustomed
Was denied them. Consequently,
Many of them who had trouble
In adjusting to the new life
Used the reservation as a
Base for forays into Texas.

V

Texas was the only homeland
Ever known by many of them.
Dispossessed and dislocated,
They were of the firm opinion
That a state of open season
Existed for all marauders
In the unprotected outlands.

In this state of wild confusion—
Soldiers occupying Phantom
While Comanches still were claimants
To the land, with Stem attempting
To bring harmony from chaos—
Circumstances forged the setting
For a classic Indian epic.

VI

The immortal bard of Avon
Never penned a more compelling
Story than the Clear Fork Valley
Witnessed when a Wichita chief
Chose to die instead of forfeit
Liberty for life in bondage.

The ingredients of drama—
Conflict, mystery, soul-searching
And displays of all the shadings
Of emotions known to humans,
Plus suspense and rapid action—
Were in evidence that blustery
March night in the seething valley.

Prairie land and stately mesas
Formed a backdrop for the staging
Of a drama without equal.
Overhead, the lights of heaven—
Moon and stars and intermittent
Prolonged lightning—dimmed and brightened
By fantastic cloud formations
Of a dozen hues and colors
Lying on the north horizon,
Were facilities for lighting.
Sound effects were rolling waters
Of the rising Clear Fork River
And the peals of distant thunder.

Music came from night winds strumming
On the thorny harps of cacti;
And from rimrocks in the background
Wolves and panthers serenaded
With a muted, mournful chorus,
Emphasizing the young chieftain's
Tragic end upon the altar
Of implacable decision.

VII

In the waning days of winter,
Wichita Chief Ko-we-a-ka

Paid a visit to the Clear Fork
Agency and told Stem that he
Came from Indian Territory
To engage Lipan Apaches.

Grown wise in ways of marauders,
Stem was satisfied the Indians
Were in Texas bent on stealing
Horses. After citing many
Cases of horse theft committed
Recently in frontier country,
Stem enlisted Ko-we-a-ka's
Help in urging that his kinsmen
Halt their thieving expeditions
And return the stolen horses.

With assurance he would aid Stem,
Ko-we-a-ka and his warriors
Left for Indian Territory.

VIII

. . . Meanwhile, Major Henry Sibley,
Commandant at Fortress Croghan,
Far southeastward from the Clear Fork,
Was chagrined by oft repeated
Raids upon his dragoon stables.

Following a theft that cost him
Nine fine mounts, the major swore that
He would put an end to horse theft.
Newton Givens was selected
To accompany Major Sibley.

Having heard of Stem's influence
With the red men, Sibley headed

Straight for Phantom Hill, then onward
To the Clear Fork River crossing
And Stem's agency for Indians.

Shortly after Sibley got there,
Ko-we-a-ka kept his promise
And returned with stolen horses.
With him were his wife, Ah-ke-ma,
And their small son Tiny Feather,
Several braves, squaws, papooses.

Fourteen horses were included
In the string that Ko-we-a-ka
Brought to Stem to be surrendered
For return to rightful owners.
Two of these mounts, it developed,
Had been stolen at Fort Croghan.

Sibley and Stem both insisted
On return of all the horses.
Ko-we-a-ka told them frankly
He had done his best to carry
Out his promise to the agent,
But that others were unwilling
To assist him. He was helpless.

IX

Out of patience, Stem and Sibley
Sought to force return of all the
Animals taken at Croghan
By arresting Ko-we-a-ka
And his party. They decided
To imprison them at Belknap.
Two of the braves would be sent for

The remainder of the horses.
Ko-we-a-ka and the others
Would, as hostages, be held there.

As the aide of Major Sibley,
Givens watched proceedings closely,
And condemned the arbitrary
Actions of both Stem and Sibley.

X

With arrest of Ko-we-a-ka,
A Pandora's box of trouble
Burst wide open, and the chieftain's
Spirit rose to meet the challenge.
Great ideals that some men live for
Also make for nobler dying.
Lives of dreamers, heroes, martyrs
Soar to starry heights unknown in
Realms of ordinary mortals.

Words cannot attain description
To delineate the depthless
Splendor of idealism
Evidenced by Ko-we-a-ka
At his rendezvous with fortune:
Savagery reversed, enthralling!

His self-sacrifice, devotion,
Love of family and freedom
Have no parallel in annals
Of Clear Fork romance or legend.
He exemplified the finest
Innate dignity of mankind
Of whatever race or credo.

227

XI

As the shades of night were falling,
Newton walked to Ko-we-a-ka's
Lodge and told him that "Tomorrow
They will take you to Fort Belknap.
Two of your braves will be sent to
Gather up remaining horses.
You and others of your party
Will be prisoners until the
Animals are brought to Belknap.

"It surpasseth understanding
On my part to see the reason
For this action. To my knowledge
There is not another chieftain
Who has volunteered assistance
In recovering stolen horses.
Surely, justice has miscarried
In this instance. I am sorry."

"My friend, let it not disturb you,"
Ko-we-a-ka answered sadly,
"The incredible misfortune
I have brought upon my brothers
Leaves me in despair, despondent;
But be certain that I will not
Bring additional degredation
To my friends and fellow tribesmen.
Wichitas are born to freedom:
Life without it is a hollow
Tarnished token, void of meaning . . .

"Worst of all, I dread the sorrow
This will bring to my Ah-ke-ma

And our young son, Tiny Feather.
They, to whom I sing my love songs,
Now must suffer for my folly."

XII

"Love, it has been said by white men,
Like religion, faith, and others,
Is a word unknown to Indians.
This is untrue, I assure you.
In the teepee of my childhood
Deep respect and love were ever
Evident betwixt my parents;
Consequently, I have always
Known what real love is and must be!

"I have worshipped the Great Spirit—
Danced my heart out at His altar;
He has sent the rain and sunshine,
Buffalo and deer and mustang.
Long He let His red-skinned children
Roam and revel through His kingdom.
Now another race has entered
His domain and He has favored
It with weapons much more powerful
Than the Indians' bows and arrows.

"We are doomed, but Ko-we-a-ka
Does not question the Great Spirit.
He has taught me faith; I trust Him
To fulfill His final purpose.
I await, with stoicism,
Destiny . . . and it is nearing!"

Newton said good-by and left him

With a final word of comfort:
"Be not heartsick, Ko-we-a-ka,
Mayhap there will be a turning
In the trail, and new horizons
Will appear to make you happy."

XIII

. . . Ko-we-a-ka called Ah-ke-ma
To his side and told her gently
Of developments, concluding:
"I have come to a decision;
I will never go to Belknap . . .

"Two trails stretch into the offing.
Both are bathed in somber shadows—
One leads forth into tomorrow . . .
And tomorrow . . . and tomorrow:
Dreary, dismal, bleak tomorrows
In the white man's loathsome prison . . .
And the other trail, the darker,
Tortuous and mystery-laden,
Leads to freedom, I shall choose it!
Death is preferable to living
Without liberty and honor!
Now has come the time for dying—
I shall leave you ere the dawning
Of another day is witnessed.
This is good-by. I have spoken."

XIV

"Never! Never! Ko-we-a-ka,
Shall you leave me! No! Ah-ke-ma,

Who has shared your joy and pleasure,
Who has known your grief and sorrow,
Will not let you go without her!
Mine the choice to share your journey
Down the trail of no returning—
You and I and Tiny Feather
Shall be joined in death forever . . .
It is better far than living
In the shadow of dishonor,
Shorn of freedom, truth and justice."

Ko-we-a-ka's admiration
For Ah-ke-ma knew no limit . . .
"You have spoken well, Ah-ke-ma,
We shall journey on together.
Death to me is not a stranger:
In the chase and on the warpath
He has passed me by quite often.
He has never seemed unfriendly;
Therefore, I dread not the journey
To the stronghold of his kingdom.
Life has shown me countless wonders;
Death will do no less, believe me.

"I who love unfettered freedom,
Love the feel of wind and sunshine,
Love the prairies and the mountains,
Animals and birds and flowers—
Love all gifts of the Great Spirit—
Cannot live within a prison.

XV

"Mine have been the heady pleasures
Of the chase, the kill, the feasting!

I have known the power and glory
Of the battle — and the victory!
Mine have been the bold adventures:
Shooting rapids, scaling dizzy
Walls of canyons stretching skyward . . .
I have downed in flight the eagle;
Ridden gleefully the surging
Waters of swift, raging rivers . . .
I have been a nameless dreamer
Roving through the scenic marvels
Of the land I love and cherish:
Endless miles of softly tinted,
Folded hills, plateaus, arroyos,
Cone-shaped mountains, placid waters;
Tangled growths of manzanita,
Cacti, chaparral, and sagebrush . . .

"Now the end of time is nearing,
I experience transition:
Hunter, home with many trophies;
Warrior, home and victory-laden;
Home, adventurer, explorer;
Home the dreamer from the mystic
Realms of fancy and enchantment;
Home, the lover to his fireside
With the fondest recollections
Known to man since day's first dawning!

"I have sipped the choicest nectar
Life can offer. Now, Ah-ke-ma,
Let us journey gladly onward
To the land of new adventure!"

. . . Ko-we-a-ka slowly doffed his

Moccasins and placed them neatly
Near the head of buckskin pallet—
Token that he would not need them
Any more . . . "There's no tomorrow
In the land where we are going,"
Softly spoke the saddened chieftain.

Then he took his knife, deep hidden,
From his leggings, felt its keenness . . .
Planted a last kiss on quivering
Lips of smiling Tiny Feather
And Ah-ke-ma . . . Plunged the dagger
Deep into the hearts of loved ones.

When his death chant, low and plaintive,
Sounded through the silent camp site,
Guards appeared to learn the meaning
Of the dirge, and Ko-we-a-ka
Flashed his knife into the midriff
Of the first one to approach him;
Second sentinel took deadly
Aim and ended Ko-we-a-ka's
Life, exactly as he planned it.

XVI

. . . Suddenly the moon was blotted
Out by storm clouds. Piercing lightning
Rent the heavens. Rolling thunder
Sharp resounded through the valley.
Rain, like tears, fell from heaven—
Cleansed the land of blood and horror.

Unexpectedly the rain clouds
Separated and the moon glow

Bathed the sweet clean earth with brightness.
Jesse Stem's swift investigation
Disclosed details of the drama:
Golden moonbeams dancing lightly
On the countenance of lovely
Indian mother made a picture
That the most exacting artist
Could but fail at reproduction.
Seven-year-old Tiny Feather,
In Ah-ke-ma's arms enfolded,
Was a portrait of contentment . . .
Innocence and trust were mirrored
On his young and peaceful features.

Nearby lay the warrior-chieftain
And the sentinel who traded
Lives to end the stirring story.

Ko-we-a-ka and his dear ones
Took the long last sleep together . . .
Happy in the child-like knowledge
They would waken some tomorrow
In a land of boundless freedom
Ruled by love and truth and justice—
Happy Hunting Ground of Indians . . .

Chapter Twenty-one

Stem's Murder

ALMOST LIKE an anti-climax
To the death of Ko-we-a-ka
Was the murder of the agent,
Stem, and a friend from Ohio.

After Jesse Stem's resignation
From the service, he engaged in
Farming on some land preempted
On the Brazos near Fort Belknap.
Stem and an Ohioan neighbor,
Lepperman by name, were making
Plans to move their wives and children
To the frontier land of Texas.

While returning from Ohio
Via Shreveport, Louisiana,
Where they had engaged a teamster
With freight wagons to haul house goods
And supplies to Belknap Village,
Stem and his friend met with foul play.

Just a few miles from Fort Belknap,
Walking toward their destination,

Following a wagon breakdown,
They were murdered, and their bodies
Mutilated. When the mystery
Was investigated by the
Military, they suspected
Wichitas had taken vengeance
For the death of Ko-we-a-ka.

II

When the blame could not be sadd'ed
On the Wichitas, Lieutenant
H. D. Tree and a contingent
Of investigators journeyed
Northward, seeking a solution
To the murder of the white men.
Captain Simmons, Fort Arbuckle
Commandant, lent his assistance.
In emergencies of this tpye
Captain Simmons called a trusted
Delaware scout named Black Beaver
Into service. It developed
That Black Beaver was familiar
With the story of the killings—
Kickapoos had killed the white men.

Captain Simmons sent for Mosqua,
Chief of Kickapoos, who told him:
"Yes, I know about the killings—
They were witnessed by a youngster
Who has told the sordid story.
So-kok-wah and Pe-a-tah-kak
Have brought shame upon their tribesmen.

We are making every effort
To arrest them. Braves are searching
For them at this very moment—
Have no fear. They shall be punished!"

III

Two days later Pe-a-tah-kak
Fell into the hands of searchers
Who returned him to the village.
Mosqua had him bound and sent him
Under heavy guard to Simmons.

On the way to Fort Arbuckle,
Pe-a-tah-kak, from concealment,
Drew a knife and cut his shackles.
As he tried to flee, his nephew
Sank a tomahawk into his
Skull. Placing the lifeless body
On a horse the braves proceeded
To Arbuckle where delivery
Of the corpse was made to Simmons.

. . . An appeal was made by Mosqua
For Sa-kok-wah's apprehension:
"Any person," stated Mosqua,
"Sighting Sa-kok-wah is ordered
To dispatch him without mercy."

At a distant Indian camp site
On the banks of the Canadian
River lived Sa-kok-wah's brother.
It was to this kinsman's teepee
That he fled in time of trouble.

"I, a fugitive from justice,"
Said, Sa-kok-wah to his brother,
"Am despised by my own people.
Like a wild beast I am hunted;
Like a deer with lance protruding
From his shoulder, sorely wounded,
I cannot escape my tribesmen.
I would have sought the protection
Of wild Indians but was fearful
Lest I starve before I reached them.
Having no where else, my brother,
I can turn, I seek the refuge
Of your teepee, knowing full well
You will not attempt to hide me."

"You are right," replied the brother.
"I have warned you times unnumbered
Of the consequence attending
Ways of life you chose to follow.
You would not abide my warning,
And my counsel you rejected.
Through your heedless, lawless actions
You have earned the foul displeasure
Of both white men and your kinsmen;
They demand full reparation
For the deeds you have committed.
It becomes my painful duty
To proclaim your life a forfeit."
With these words the brother lifted
High his tomahawk and slew him.

When the chief got information
Of the deed he called a council.

As the distance to Arbuckle
Was too great for transportation
Of the body, head was severed
And delivered to the fortress
So the officer commanding
Could substantiate the story.

Thus the murders of the former
Indian agent and companion
Were avenged in forthright manner
By the Kickapoos in striving
To adjust to laws of white men.

Randolph Marcy summed it this way:

" . . . Justice of the Kickapoo tribe
Is astounding and evinces
A regard for law and order . . .
And . . . inflexibility of
Spirit in the execution
Of its mandates seldom followed
Among any race of people."

Chapter Twenty-two

Phantom Hill Legends

FROM FORT CROGHAN Givens managed,
With the help of Colonel Lovelace,
To be transferred to Fort Phantom,
Nearest fortress to the ranch site.
As the mule teams slowly plodded
Toward the post upon the Clear Fork,
Newton and Lucinda gaily
Talked about the Clear Fork Valley.

"Phantom Hill . . . its name . . how haunting,"
Mused Lucinda. "It has always
Conjured visions sharp and vivid
Of some sad and somber romance . . .
Or a tragedy of some sort . . .
Or . . . perhaps . . . a melodrama . . .
Won't you tell me of its naming?"

Newton fell into a pensive
Mood and groped for a beginning:
"No one seems to know exactly
Where the appellation came from.
Native lore is rife with legends—

Every one of them intriguing—
From which one might choose an answer.

"It is said that in the early
Days the phantomland abounded
With illusive and elusive
Wonders — all of them mirages:
Pixilated Indians visioned
Forests, grasslands, pools of water,
Villages and game and other
Fantasies where nought existed.

"And another ancient folk tale,
Rising from the mist of ages
Long since dead, relates the horror
Of fanaticism practiced
By a tribe of red-skinned heathens:
Periodically the Aztecs
Came from lands far south to worship
Their Great Spirit and to offer
Hapless human sacrifices
On their fiery pagan altars.

"Surely this is superstition
Pure and simple! Notwithstanding,
When a blood-red moon creeps slowly
Over far-off hills at midnight,
Credence to the tale is lent by
Winds that hum low, mournful music
And by moaning, muted voices
Drifting clearly and distinctly
From the realms of bygone ages:
Sadness-burdened, plaintive voices

Of lost souls condemned to wander
Evermore as nameless phantoms
On a non-existent hilltop . . .

Superstition also narrates
That, in times of old, suspected
Violators of the tribal
Laws of certain long-lost people
Found a haven on the Phantom,
Similar to refuge cities
In Old Testament recorded . . .

"In the dim and early ages,
Runs an interesting tradition,
Solemn, sacred, secret powwows
Between sorcerers and Indian
Gods and goddesses were held here . . .

"Most romantic of the legends
Tells how Phantom Hill was fashioned
As a place for the confinement
Of a banished Spanish lover.

"In the heyday of their glory,
When Comanches, gay and carefree,
Were the lords of Texas rangelands—
So the fascinating legend
Says — when bold *conquistadores*
Crossed the plains in search of golden
Treasure, one was lost and wandered
Into a Comanche village.
It is said he was a favorite
Member of the royal household,
Kinsman of the Spanish ruler.
"Ere a moon had passed, the Spaniard

Stole the heart of Princess Blue Sky,
Daughter of the greatest chieftain
Ever known to the Comanches.
"Ardently the charming princess
Pled their cause before her father.
But the chieftain would not sanction
Marriage to the *caballero*.

"At long last the great chief counseled
With his sorcerers and shamans.
'You are all aware,' he told them,
'Of the love my daughter fosters
For the stranger in our village.
I have contemplated many
Ways of dealing with the matter,
None of which is satisfactory.

" 'It would be unwise to slay him;
This would surely serve to sever
The affection that my daughter
Has for me. I long to keep it;
I prefer to see him banished
From the kingdom of Comanches
To a distant land of exile
From whence there is no returning.
Time will heal the sorely wounded
Heart of Blue Sky; then an Indian
Brave will come to make her happy.
One of you must find an answer
To the problem that besets me.'

"Spake an old sagacious sachem:
'Medicine I make is stronger
Than the medicine of others!

I shall create for my chieftain
A disappearing hill, a phantom,
Unattainable to all men
Save the ones I place upon it.

" 'There, my great chief may be certain
Princess Blue Sky's zealous lover
Will be captive till the rivers
Flow no more and mighty mountains
Crumble in the dust of eons.

" 'That the young man may not perish,
Fill a *travois* with provisions
That need never be replenished
As my medicine will make them
Inexhaustible and keep them
Always fresh and appetizing.

" 'You must bear in mind, however,
Whosoever is committed
To vicinity of Phantom
Hill, confinement is forever.
No man can undo the magic
Of the spell once it is fashioned.
I have spoken!' Said the chieftain:

" 'I accept the plan. 'Tis perfect!
On the morrow I shall journey
Toward the sunrise on a hunting
Expedition. After two days
Take a *travois* to the teepee
Of the Spaniard and abduct him.
Hide him well with robes and blankets,
That the princess may not see him.

Take him forthwith to the country
Of the Phantom Hill and leave him
To his fate of endless exile.'

" . . . Princess Blue Sky, picking flowers
On the day of the abduction,
Pondered on a premonition
That some unforeseen and dreadful
Evil hovered in the offing.
Intuition seemed to guide her
Toward the teepee of the sachem.
She approached her destination
Cautiously and watched the sachem
Load the *travois* with provisions.
As she watched, the sachem covered
The supplies with robes and blankets;
Then he drove the *travois* swiftly
To the teepee of her sweetheart.

"Suddenly she sensed the meaning
Of the wily sachem's actions.
When he went into the teepee
For the Spaniard, Princess Blue Sky,
Hesitating not an instant,
Slipped the bonds of tribal training,
Climbed beneath the colored blankets,
Pressed her body, small and slender,
Hard against the packed provisions.
Breathlessly she waited, fearful
Lest the sachem hear the pounding
Of her heart and put an end to
Her resolve to share the fortune—
Whether it be good or evil—
She had chosen with her lover.

"Blue Sky heard belabored footsteps
As the sachem brought the spellbound
Spaniard to the laden *travois*,
Carefully and quickly tucking
Him beneath the outspread covers.
Sachem never once suspected
The addition to his cargo.

"In a spacious, sparkling, splendorous
Land of lovely lavish landscapes
The sachem halted his *travois*,
Cast anew his spell and hastened
Back to the Comanche village.

"This according to the legend,
Was the origin of Phantom
Hill, the home of Princess Blue Sky
And her royal-blooded sweetheart.

"To this good day, says tradition,
In ecstatic bliss they wander
Arm in arm across the ages—
Happy exiles on a hilltop
Often seen but never reached by
Ordinary earth-bound mortals.

"It could be that there is truth in
Some or all of the traditions,
But regardless of the legends—
True or untrue does not matter—
Phantom Hill is aptly labeled:
Due to optical illusion,
The mystic mound, from a distance,
Seems to be an elevation

Well above surrounding country.
When the height is gained, however,
It has disappeared — the Phantom
Eases into level stretches."

"What a lovely lot of legends,"
Happily exclaimed Lucinda.
"And the way you told them, darling,
Is romantic and convincing . . .
Tell me more about this fabled
Land . . . And of Fort Phantom's founding."

II

"While a monument to Indian
Fancy, folklore, and tradition,"
Newton pondered and continued,
"History also is a claimant
Of the Hill and its environs.
Aye, the Phantom is a factual
Monument to the initial
Military installation
In the valley of the Clear Fork
Of the storied Brazos River.

"Founding of the fort involves a
Lot of romance and tradition
That dates back to prehistoric
Times — before the white man's advent,
And a vast array of events
That have transpired since his coming.
I fear all of this may bore you."

"No, indeed," Lucinda answered,
"It is thrilling! I adore it!"

Newton's furrowed brow announced that
He was having difficulty
Picking up a thread for spinning
The enchanting and revealing
Story of the frontier region.

III

" . . . Verily, *Comancheria*
Was, and is, a paradoxal
World of many moods and markings
Where the fierce horse-borne Comanche
Rides in wild wind-blown abandon.
Passages of stark labrynthic
Detail interlace its sprawling
Limits — game lanes, trailways, warpaths.

"So deep in *Comancheria*
Sink the roots of legendary
Tartars of the Plains that folklore
And tradition give no inkling
Of their birthing or fruition.

"What has been described by Marcy
As the Westland's 'Great Zahara,'
Uninviting and unwanted
By the westward pushing settlers,
Is, in part, an Indian Eden,
Flush with all things necessary
To the savage life that thrives here.
I have crossed *Comancheria*
Several times. I know it varies
From a wasteland starved and lonely
To a paradise of plenty.

"When the Spaniards and the Frenchmen
First explored the spacious empire,
They were challenged by Comanches
And, no doubt, would have been slaughtered
Had their weapons not been better
Than the Indian's bows and lances.

"While less savage tribes of red men
Labored with *Franciscan* friars
In the building of their missions,
The Comanches rode the war trails
Firm in their age old conviction
That it was their bounden duty
To annihilate intruders
On their rich and spreading birthright.

"Palettes, brushes, paints, and mixtures
In the hands of ardent artists
Could not capture in a hundred
Years the grandeur and the glory
Of the wondrous monumental
Magic of this macroscopic
Universe — *Comancheria!*

"There are no words for extolling
Vivid virtues and attractions
Of this fabulous, exciting
Land of color, contrast, challenge:
Lonely land of sun and silence
Where the evanescent glimmer
Of the sunlight and the shadows
Lend enchantment to the secrets
Of the *terra incognita*.

Friendly land of happy chatter
As the duties of the household
Are performed by happy women;
Laughing land of noisy children
Playing in a teepee village.

"Land of dreary desolation:
Sandy gulches, deep arroyos;
World of desert growth abundant;
Greasewood, ocotillo, yucca,
And a hundred other hardy
Plants peculiar to the badlands.

"Land of stately oaks outspreading,
Cedar brakes and virgin forests.
Land of glowing, golden promise:
Lofty mountains, free for scaling;
Trails that lead to great adventure;
Nameless rivers — all inviting
Navigation, irrigation,
And a life of virgin plenty.
Land of fiery, fearsome beauty:
Barren wastes and blinding sandstorms;
World of rare breath-taking glitter,
Land of glowing scenic wonders—
Land of crazy contradictions!"

Chapter Twenty-three

Meeting of the Races

AS THE LITTLE train of wagons—
Givens family and their escorts—
Ambled onward toward Fort Phantom,
Newton went on with his story:

" . . . Early meetings of Comanches
With Americans were cordial;
The frail, fickle hand of friendship
Was extended by both races.
But perversities of earthlings
Soon changed feelings into mutual
Hatred of the toughest texture.
Searching for an explanation
Of this odd, obtuse reversal
Of respect for one another
Leads one only to confusion:
Inexplicable, it dates back
To a sad misunderstanding
Between brothers Cain and Abel
In the far grey dawn of history.

II

"Five events of rapid moving
Times have basically influenced

Current status of the region:
Revolution, annexation,
Mexican War, immigration,
Finding gold in California.

III

"Tragedy is no newcomer
To the land of Northwest Texas.
Back when Houston was preparing
For the fight at San Jacinto,
Agents of the government of
Mexico appeared among the
Kiowas-Comanches bearing
Gifts of weapons, ammunition;
And suggested that much plunder
Might be taken from the homesteads
Of the men engaged in fighting
In the Texas Revolution.
This was all the invitation
Needed by embittered red men,
Fearful of encroaching settlers.

IV

"Texas refugees were fleeing
Northward in increasing numbers;
The Comanches went to meet them.
On the fourteenth day of April,
Eigtheen Thirty-six, a party
Of nine men and three young children
Were massacred by the Indians.
Mrs. Horn and Mrs. Harris,

Widows of two of the murdered
Men, were captured and subjected
To the heartless, brutish treatment
Meted out to enslaved women.
Other depredations followed.

"Eighteen Thirty-six, in Maytime,
Cynthia Parker and her brother,
Children of a Texas Ranger,
Were among the captives taken,
Following the gory, gruesome
Butchery at Parker's Fortress
On the Navasota River.

V

"With their prisoners and pillage,
The Comanches started westward
Toward the *Llano Estacado*.
First night out they held a scalp dance
To commemorate their victory.
When they neared the Caprock country,
In the *Valles de las Grinas,**
Indians halted and apportioned
To the bands participating,
Plunder taken in the foray—
After which the tribes divided.
Such scenes were repeated often
As the borderland crept westward.

VI

"On the warpath the Comanche
Is a demon dedicated

* Valley of Tears

To his enemy's destruction.
But it is a different picture
In his home upon the prairie.
There, I've found, he is a person
Far removed from abject savage:
Bound in ritual, his real life
Is quite often contemplative.
It is true his culture, customs,
Practices, beliefs, traditions
Differ widely from the white man's.
Yet I've found him, when permitted,
To possess a sense of justice
And humility which staggers
That portrayed by many white men.

VII

"Let me add a little side light
To the Cynthia Parker story:
Once while scouting for the colonel,
Lone Coyote took me to the
Camp of Chief Peta Nocona.
'Peta's wife,' said Lone Coyote,
'Is the long-lost Cynthia Parker.'

"Blond and blue-eyed, she was lovely.
In a talk with her she told me
She was happy beyond measure;
Could in no wise be persuaded
To forsake adopted tribesmen
And return to her own people.

"I have also known of cases
Where white boys by Indians captured

Have succumbed to tribal customs
And refused to be delivered.
Some have been rescued or ransomed
Only to make every effort
To return to their adopted
Kinsmen in *Comancheria*.

VIII

" . . . When the Lone Star joined the Union,
Texans felt that frontier troubles
Soon would end and Indian raiders
Would be dealt with by the federal
Troops in no uncertain manner.
Such was not the case, however.
Actually, a triple system
Of defense was ineffective:
State and federal troops were bolstered
By determined frontier Texans
Who would organize in posses
For their mutual protection.

"Early Eighteen Forty-six found
War with Mexico impendent.
Naturally the war played havoc
With defense of Northwest Texas.
Troop withdrawals from the frontier
Gave the red men an advantage
They were quick to grasp, and raiding,
Pillaging, marauding, murder
Formed their old familiar pattern.

"That was when the dragoons journeyed
To South Texas where they coupled

Forces with General Taylor."

"I remember," sighed Lucinda.

"I went on across the border
To participate in battles
Of Resaca de la Palma,
Monterrey and Palo Alto,
Buena Vista, Cerro Gordo,
And some half a dozen other
Skirmishes of no importance.

"There I learned the 'yell of Texas'—
Combination Indian war whoop
And a plaintive call for cattle:
It starts with a low bass rumble,
Rises in ghost-like crescendo
To a frenzied shriek of horror
Capable of striking terror
In the hearts of all who hear it.
It goes something on this order . . . "

Here Lucinda interrupted:
"I have heard it. Don't repeat it!
I agree that it is dreadful.
Please continue with your story."

" . . . By mid Eighteen Forty-seven
Governor Henderson succeeded
In putting through a plan for rangers
To be paid with federal money.
Thus nine companies of rangers
Formed a new frontier-protecting
Line extending from Cooke County
To the gulf coast — Corpus Christi.

"When the war was over, we, the
Second Regiment of Dragoons,
Were assigned to help establish
Forts to replace ranger stations.

IX

"Simultaneous with ending
Of the war was the discovery
Of gold in far California.

"Gold has ever played important
Roles in man's march through the ages.
It seemed destined to assist in
Wresting the *Comancheria*
From its fervent red defenders.
California, Arizona,
And New Mexico were mining
Gold before James William Marshall
Found his dusky yellow nugget
In the mill race of John Sutter's
Sawmill in late January,
Eighteen Hundred and Forty-eight.

"When the cry of 'gold!' resounded
Through the hills of California,
It re-echoed till the message
Carried far across the nation.

"Am I boring you with details?"
Inquired Newton. "No, my dearest,
I am happily digesting
Every word. It's fascinating!
Your accumulated knowledge

Of a land so new and youthful
That it has no written history
Leaves me in a state of wonder.

"Clear Fork Valley holds our future
So I naturally am eager
To know everything about it.
I shall never tire of listening
To events that shaped its gripping
Past. Of course, I know the present
And look forward to the future—
But for now go right on telling
Me the saga of the Clear Fork,
Mr. Givens, I am waiting!'

"Yes, ma'am," Newton smiled and kissed her.
"Where was I? Oh, yes, the gold rush!"

Newton fired his pipe, proceeding:
"The new mania, gold fever,
Soared to epidemic stages,
And a mighty tide of restless
Fortune hunters headed westward.

X

"Within a year, Forty-Niners,
Argonauts, and kindred spirits
Flooded every route of travel
Known, and opened countless new trails:
In the history of mankind
There is not a parallel to
The mad rush to California.

"As the tide of immigration

Rolled across Comanche homelands,
The intrusion brought displeasure
To the Indians, and they challenged
Threats to their ancestral domain.

"Many of the smaller parties,
Reckless men with insufficient
Means of travel and equipment,
Never reached the land of promise.
Graves by thousands dot the trailways
Through the land of the Comanches,
Left unmarked, unwept, unnoticed.

"Since their land was penetrated
And its secrets known to others,
The Comanches, long unconquered,
Faced a desperate situation . . .
In bewilderment they gazed on
Screeching, toiling covered wagons
Rolling in increasing numbers
Farther west across their prairies.

"Even with the antiquated
Means of defense of Comanches,
I predict that long and costly
Wars will be fought for possession
Of the land, but it is certain
In the end white men will claim it.

"With establishment of outposts
Far across the restless border,
The advancement of the frontier
Has begun in deadly earnest.
But Comanches are a worthy

Foe on any field of battle—
And let no man tell you different.

XI

"Slowly, painfully the westward
Movement seemed to creep by inches.
Eighteen Fifty found the frontier
Plagued by fury, fear, and frenzy.
Palls of dread of fierce and hostile
Indians hung across the country
From Red River to the gulflands.
Federal and state officials
Were beseiged by protestations
And petitions seeking succor
From the fuming, flaring fury
Of the red man's bitter struggle
To retain his treasured homeland.

"Once again the military,
State and national, took action.
Colonel William Hardee led us—
Second Dragoons — in a campaign
To annihilate defenders
Of immense *Comancheria*.
Ranger Captains Big Foot Wallace,
J. S. Ford, and John J. Grumbles
Lent their full support to Hardee.
Combined efforts of the forces
Failed to weaken the position
Of Comancheland defenders.

XII

"Depredations unabated,
Top officials of the army
Studied plans and set in motion
New approaches to the problem
Of defending frontier Texas.

"Our return with Randolph Marcy
From Santa Fe by Dona Ana
Led us through Comanche country.
Marcy recommended building
Army posts throughout the region
That would serve the dual purpose
Of protecting immigration
On the road to California
And preventing molestation
Of the settlers in the outlands.

"His proposal now was sanctioned
And the plan put into action . . .
We, my dear, are now approaching
One of those posts." Newton pointed
Toward a distant group of buildings:
"There, Lucinda, is Fort Phantom!"

Chapter Twenty-four

Growing Herds

WHILE LUCINDA and the children
Rested from the lengthy journey,
Newton, taking David with him,
Rode out to the ranch to visit
Edwin and to check the livestock.

He was pleased to note great increase
In the number of the cattle,
Sheep, and horses. Edwin told him
That the hounds had long since become
Expert in the chase of quarry.

As they talked, a stalwart horseman
Rode up. Edwin introduced him:
"This is Pah-hah-yo-ko, Newton.
Clear Fork Valley is a favorite
Campground of his band of northern
Comanches, the Yamparikas.
They come to the valley often
To hunt buffalo and powwow
With the friendly Indian agent
Who assists them with their problems

And is generous with presents.

"Pah-hah-yo-ko is a master
Teacher in the ways of wildlife.
He has taught me many secrets
Of the fox and wolf and panther.

"In our zestful hunts together,
A fine friendship has developed—
Deep respect exists between us.
The hounds seem to fascinate him,
And he is a tireless hunter.

"It is said that on the warpath
He is an outstanding leader.
I have learned that Clear Fork Valley
Is at peace when he is near it—
I am grateful for his friendship."

"Yes," said Newton, "Yamparikas
Are a fearsome tribe of warriors.
Other Indians don't molest them."

"Ugh," responded Pah-hah-yo-ko
As he loped off on his pony.
"That means everything or nothing,"
Edwin laughed. "Now getting back to
What I was about to say when
Pah-hah-yo-ko interrupted.

"This is truly livestock country.
The herds have increased much faster
Than I had anticipated.
For example, take the cattle:
In addition to the calf crops,

I have purchased several head from
Indians passing through the country.
I suspect that they were stolen
But no one has come to claim them.
And a few drift in from somewhere—
Maybe Indian Territory,
Maybe settlements to eastward.

"Anyway, we need a market
For twelve hundred head. Fort Phantom
And Fort Belknap quartermasters
Buy a few along, but we are
Getting more than we can handle."

"Have you thought of California?"
Newton asked. "I hear South Texas
Ranchers make the drive. The profits
Are tremendous. I have learned that
Good steers bring two hundred dollars
In the California gold camps.
Certainly, the risks are heavy.
Indians and the natural terrain
Pose a hundred knotty problems,
But with careful preparation
And enough men one can make it."

"Kansas City and Chicago,
Edwin said, "are also markets.
I had contemplated talking
With you about driving cattle
North, but, frankly, California
Is a new idea. Prices
There are five times higher . . .

Are you sure your information
Is correct?" "I'm sure," said Newton.

"What would be my route of travel?"
Questioned Edwin. "Take the Marcy
Trail," said Newton. "You remember
It, I'm certain. At El Paso
Take the trail the others follow.

"You will need to get equipment
And a crew of men together.
I would take at least six wagons
And three dozen topnotch drovers.
You will need sufficient oxen,
Ammunition, bed rolls, foodstuff.
I can help you get the wagons
And supplies at Phantom, Belknap.
Can you manage for the drovers?"

"I can get them," Edwin answered.
"It will take a bit of doing
And some traveling . . . but I'll get them.
And I want to start as soon as
Possible — to take advantage
Of the spring rains; we will need them."

"Aye, you're right," responded Newton.

Chapter Twenty-five

Trail Drive

IT WAS LATE in February
When their plans were made for making
The trail drive to California.

Edwin had accepted Newton's
Offer of help in acquiring
Wagons and supplies at Belknap
And Fort Phantom. Next day Edwin
Told his foreman Pilgrim Proffet
Of the plans and of his promise
To get drovers for the trail drive.

"You have quite a job," said Pilgrim.
"Where do you propose to get them?"

"Well," said Edwin, "the Cross Timbers,
Peters Colony, and Birdville
Might supply them, but I doubt it."

"San Antonio," said Pilgrim,
"Is the surest place of finding
Good cow hands. The only trouble
Is it takes so long to get there."

"I am anxious to get started,"
Edwin stated. "I'll try Austin
First, and if it's necessary
I'll go on to San Antonio.
I would like to take Slim Nelson
With me. You will be short handed,
But I think that you can manage."

"I can make it fine," said Pilgrim.
"Boggs and Morgan are returning
From Fort Belknap in the morning—
And there's always Pah-hah-yo-ko . . . "

"No remarks about my sidekick,"
Edwin grinned, and started packing.

II

Making final preparations,
Edwin said to Slim, "Be ready
To depart at daybreak. We will
Spend tomorrow night at Phantom."
. . . At Fort Phantom they were welcomed
By Lucinda and the children.
Shortly Newton came in laughing:
"Well, you lost no time in getting
Here. I guess you're after drovers;
You will find none at Fort Phantom!"

"How I wish I could," said Edwin.
He revealed his plans to Newton,
Who approved them. "Fortunately,"
Newton said, "I found four wagons
And some thirty head of oxen

They are surplus here at Phantom.
I have made a bid to buy them.
Since there are no other bidders
It is certain I will get them.
And I learned that other wagons
Are available at Belknap.

As they chatted after supper,
Newton said, "A wagon master,
Thomas Shelton, contracts hauling
From the Austin Army Depot.
If there are cow hands in Austin
He can find them. You should see him."

III

Down the military roadway
Slim and Edwin paced their horses.
In three days they were in Austin.

"Yes," said Shelton, "I can help you.
There's a man named Calvin Brewster
Who returned last month from making
A trail drive to California.
And there are a dozen other
Cowboys doing winter odd jobs
Who would welcome full employment."

In a talk with Calvin Brewster
Edwin learned that Bronco Bailey
Had been trail boss on the long trek.

"Do you know where I can find him?
Can I hire him?" questioned Edwin.

"He is visiting his cousin
Anson Jones, at Independence.
You might hire him," Brewster answered.
"Several of the trail hands wintered
With kinsfolk at Independence,"
Added Brewster. "We will go there,"
Stated Edwin. "Get your bedroll.
Meet me at the livery stable."

"Slim," said Edwin, "I believe that
It would be well for you to take
The men I've hired to the Clear Fork.
Go by Phantom for the wagons
And the oxen. I am certain
Newton will have made arrangements
For the balance of equipment
From Fort Belknap. You will get it.
Take it to the ranch. Tell Pilgrim
To have wagons and the cattle
Ready by the time I get there.
I am going to Independence;
Calvin Brewster will go with me.
We will be along as soon as
I complete the crew of drovers."

IV

As they cantered down the roadway,
Brewster talked about the city
They were rapidly approaching:
"Independence is the 'Athens
Of Texas,' a solid, thriving
Town of culture, education,

Commerce, government, religion;
Many noted Texans live there.

"Baylor University for
Men is a great institution.
Baylor College is for women,
They are the best schools in Texas."

They were now within the townsite.
It was Sunday. Brewster pointed
Out the homes of many persons
Who were prominent in Texas.
As they passed the church, the people
Visited before departing
In their buggies, surreys, horseback.

"The man talking with the preacher
Is Sam Houston who was twice the
President of the Republic,"
Brewster said. "And there is Anson!
Hold my horse while I go ask him
If he knows where we can locate
Bronco. I'll just be a minute."

When he came back, Brewster stated:
"He is at the Jones' plantation."

The plantation, a short distance
From the town, was quite impressive.
The main house, a stately structure,
Was often referred to as "The
Last White House of the Republic."

V

"Hi, there, Brewster!" shouted Bailey
From an open upstairs window.

"Y'all have chairs on the veranda.
I'll be down in just a minute."

After introductions, Edwin
Told the purpose of his visit
To Bronco and asked if he would
Take the trail boss job and help him
Finish out a crew of drovers.

"It's a long old trail," sighed Bronco.
"And the challenges are many:
The nerve-wracking and exhausting
Journey brims with constant dangers.
There are rattlesnakes, mustangers,
Indians, cyclones, mean stream crossings,
Wild stampedes, and fiery tempers
Of the tired, trail-weary cow hands . . . "

Bronco paused in retrospection
While the memories of daring
Desert wastes and mountain passes
Pulled him westward like a lodestar
Toward bizarre and brutal beauty
Of grotesquely gleaming landscapes
Filled with an accursed enchantment—
Unexplainable, but certain.

Pensively Bronco commented:
"Yes, I'll take the job. There's no way
I can turn it down. We will start
Just as soon as we eat dinner.
I believe that we can manage
To complete the crew by sundown.
We can leave here in the morning

And be on the trail by Friday."
"I admire your optimistic
Outlook," Edwin said. The dinner
Bell was ringing in the courtyard.

VI

Bronco Bailey's apt prediction
Came true. Friday noon the cattle
And the slowly moving wagons
Headed out of Clear Fork Valley.

"It will be our aim," said Bronco,
"In the first few days of travel
To drive hard and keep the cattle
From stampeding and returning
To their native range." The drovers
Fresh and eager, stood their double
Guard at night without complaining.

Sunday night, with longhorns bedded
Down a few miles from Fort Phantom,
Newton rode up to the camp site.
"Scouts informed me you would be here,"
He told Edwin. "I am glad that
You made such good time in starting
The drive." "That is due," said Edwin,
"To our trail boss Bronco Bailey.
Come here, Bronco, meet my partner."

Drovers sought their bedrolls early
To get rest before their turn at
Riding night herd. Near the dwindling
Campfire, Newton talked with Edwin:
"Things are changing fast at Phantom.

272

I am in command, and rumor
Says the fort will be abandoned
At an early date. Lucinda
And the children are en route to
New Orleans. David is with them.
I wish it were possible for
Me to join you on the trail drive,
But it's not." He handed Edwin
A thick money belt. "Expenses
Will be heavy. You may need this.
It is late. I must be going."

VII

. . . Early morning, sixth of April,
Eighteen Fifty-four, the order
For abandonment was given.
Shortly afternoon the troopers,
Bound for Eagle Pass, were leaving.

Givens tarried at the fortress
To conclude reports . . . intending
To join soldiers and slow-moving
Wagons at the evening camp site.

As the sun was dipping westward,
The Comanches came by hundreds.
It was obvious that they had
Watched the post's evacuation
And had come posthaste to claim it
As a trophy won by default.

VIII

Watching, entranced from the office,
Givens witnessed the strange prelude

273

To an epic conflagration:
A bedraggled, yet imposing
Chief stood on a stoop at sunset
And addressed his people thusly:
"We are vanishing Comanches.
Dread diseases spread by white men—
Smallpox, typhoid, rheumatism,
Veneral disease, consumption—
Endless wars and bounty hunters
Have reduced our tribal numbers
To the point that there is danger
Of extinction for our people.

"Time was when we were the greatest
Warriors, raiders, hunters, horsemen
Of the plainsland. Then the paleface
Ground our fortitude and valor
Into dust and we will never
Rise again . . . But we can surely
Burn this ugly, hated symbol
Of encroachment as a token
Of defiance . . . It is certain
We can never win the conflict
With the white man; that was settled
When we lost the priceless vision
Of our fathers. We no longer
Hold the title to our birthright—
Lords of the *Comancheria*
Are reduced to pawns of white men.

"Take the torches I have fashioned
And apply them to the buildings.
As revenge it is a sorry

Measure, but tonight we dance the
Dance to memory of other
Days when we were called *The People.*
We shall dance it to the burning
Of the menace that has robbed us
Of our heritage and future.
Light the torches! Fire the buildings!
Dance! Dance! Dance! Your chief has spoken."

Slowly, through protective shadows,
Newton edged his way from office
To the stable. He led Beauty
To a safe retreat and lingered
To behold the flaming, whirling
Inferno - extravaganza . . .
At the burning he was mindful
Of the graphic Dantesque features
Of the god of fire consuming
His enormous Phantom banquet.

To the music of the crashing
Walls, which reached a mad crescendo,
Smoke danced halfway up to heaven
On the rungs of wispy ladders
Fashioned from the flames that transformed
Post on Clear Fork of the Brazos
To a mound of pale gray ashes.

After witching hours of watching,
Newton headed Beauty campward . . .
Tiny hints of dawn were birthing
Far beyond the eastern mesas.

Once he paused upon a hillock
To gaze backward . . . In the faint glow

Of the smouldering heaps of rubble,
He could see the pirouetting
Indians rapt in celebration
Of their empty, awesome victory.

IX

Riding onward, he was thinking:
"Now the time has come for building
Strong new structures in the valley;
Time to build my Ranch of Some Day—
Where the smell of wind is balsam
To the heart when one is weary;
Where the flowers, birds and wildlife
Speak serenely of well-being;
Where the voice of nature beckons
Man to mountain tops of splendorous
Realms of noblest aspirations;
Where the sunset's overflowing
Colors splash the falling curtain
Of the day with all the dazzling
Shades and blendings of the spectrum;
Where the swing of stars in heaven
Steer the soul to tranquil moments
Of communion with one's Maker;
Where my heart shall dwell forever—
Home in magic Clear Fork Valley!"

When the troopers reached Fort Duncan
At Eagle Pass on the border,
Newton was surprised at finding
Colonel Lovelace waiting for him.
He was making an inspection

Of the frontier forts. The colonel
Said that Newton was to join him
As his aide. When the inspections
Were completed, they would journey
On a furlough to New Orleans.

"No, if I can get a furlough
I am going to California
With the trail herd Edwin's taking
There to market," Newton told him.

"In that case, a leave of absence
Is what you will need," the colonel
Said. "I think I can arrange it."

X

On the heels of his departure
For El Paso came an order
For Givens to join a party,
Under Marcy's supervision,
To locate some reservations
Ordered by the legislature.
"I will go myself," the colonel
Mused. "I do not have the heart to
Send a courier for Newton:
He has earned his leave of absence."

XI

. . . During the next month stampeding
Cattle tried the nerves and patience
Of the motley crew of drovers,
Some of whom were shiftless drifters;

But the bulk of whom were honest
Men, full capable of dealing
With the trials and the hardships
Of the long and troublous cow trail
Stretching west to California.
Bridled, saddled, the night horses
Were kept handy, always ready
For a stampede that could happen
Instantly. The rapid firing
Of three shots from a revolver
Was agreed on as a signal
That the herd was on a rampage.

In the daytime, cattle easing
Down the rough trail might be startled
By an almost unseen movement
Of a deer or jackass rabbit
Into a stampede. A single
Frightened snorting steer could trigger
A maelstrom of swirling cattle.

Bronco Bailey was a master,
When he was nearby, at stopping
A stampede when it first started:
He would ride close to the leader
Forcing it into a massive
Circle. All the other cattle
Followed. Gradually the circle
Lessened in circumference and
Finally the steers were forced to
Slow into a pulsing standstill.

XII

" . . . We should reach the Pecos River

By nightfall," said Bronco Bailey
On a darksome Sunday morning.
"We must ride close herd. The cattle
Have been two days without water.
They are restless and the weather
Is uncertain. Storms or any
Of a dozen things could fetch us
A stampede. We must be watchful."

In late afternoon the thirsty
Cattle caught the scent of water
And rushed pell-mell toward the river.

Having drunk their fill, the longhorns
Settled down to anxious grazing.

When the wagons were positioned
And the cook was cooking supper,
Bronco noticed other campers
A short distance up the river.
Riding to the camp site, Bronco
Found a large crew of horse hunters
With a herd of several hundred
Mustangs heading for South Texas.

XIII

By the campfire eating supper,
Young Mike Miller said to Bronco:
"I rode over to the horse camp
After you returned. I never
Knew there were as many mustangs
As they have. I tried to question
Them about how they had captured

Such a large herd, but they wouldn't
Talk with me. They were unfriendly."

"Yes," said Bronco, "they're secretive.
They are tough and do not welcome
Company of decent *hombres*.
In a real sense they resemble
The wild horses that they deal in.

"Mustang camps are an attraction
To the fugitive and shady
Characters of several nations.
They enjoy the bold adventures
Offered by their wild profession.
While ostensibly they search for
Mustangs to recruit depleted
Herds of Mexicans and Texans,
Some of them are highway robbers,
Prairie pirates bent on seizing
Property of all descriptions.

"Often they disguise as Indians,
Leaving marks of the Comanche
On the wagon trains and ranches
And the villages they plunder.

XIV

"Mustangs are degraded cast-offs
Of some noble breeds of horses.
One may trace their equine lineage
Back to well-bred Barb or Moorish
Steeds brought here by early Spaniards.
Through their years of outcast living

They have come to be as wild as
Buffaloes, and much more vicious.
Their propensity for wildness
Is well known and runs their value
Down to fractions of the prices
Paid for improved stock. But buyers
Are plentiful. Mustang hunting
Is a thriving, paying business."

When the fire had burned to ashes,
Night herd riders sang their lonely
Songs to keep the cattle quiet,
But their songs were ineffective.
Instead of bedding down, the cattle
Milled and clashed horns — were uneasy.
Suddenly a clap of thunder
Rent the air — a stampede started.

Straight the plunging longhorns headed
For the horse camp up the river.
Three shots pierced the inky blackness
And the roar of hoofs resounded
Like an avalanche unleashing
Its mad fury on the plainsland.

Bronco sped to warn mustangers
And they gained their mounts and scattered.
When the longhorns reached the mustangs,
There was bedlam, panic, horror.
Longhorns spooked the wary mustangs
And the mustangs added madness
To the flight of fearful cattle.
They became a churning mixture

Of infuriated demons.

. . . Miles away longhorns and mustangs
Scattered into groups of milling
Animals, spent to exhaustion—
Dead ones lay upon the prairie.

At daybreak the weary cowboys
And the cursing wild horse hunters
Started the long task of rounding
Up the groups and strays and sorting
Out the mustangs from the cattle.
Gradually they reassembled
Them into respective trail herds.

Chapter Twenty-six

West of the Pecos

TWO WEEKS WESTWARD from the Pecos
The trail crossed a sandy creek bed.
"We will noon here," stated Bronco,
And see if we can find water.
You will notice," He told Edwin,
That the sand is damp in places."

Scooping out a hole, a trickle
Of cool water shortly filled it.
"It is not far to the source of
Fresh spring water. We must find it."

After eating, Bronco ordered:
"Slater, you and Riley ride up
The creek. See if you can locate
Water. We will graze the cattle."

A short distance up the winding
Creek bed, Riley called to Slater:
"Here is a small spring. And yonder,
In the recess of that shallow
Valley, I can see a tree top."

Riding up the smallish valley
Something like a mile from camp site,

The men found a spring sufficient
To take care of all the livestock,
By watering it in small bunches.

They camped in the grassy hollow
Three days greasing wagons, mending
Harness, saddles, shoeing horses,
Washing garments, shaving, resting.

From this point into El Paso
The drive settled into routine
Events: intermittent flare-ups
Of temper by touchy drovers,
An alarm or two when Indians
Were encountered, and a couple
Of stampedes, but no real trouble.

II

It was middle June when Givens
Reached El Paso. He found lodging
And began anxious inquiries
To determine if the trail herd
Had arrived. No information
Was obtainable. He waited.
Two days later a contingent
Of soldiers en route to Yuma
Arrived. They were led by Captain
Sands, an old friend from Fort Towson.
Sands told Newton of his passing
Edwin and the herd on Tuesday.
They should reach El Paso shortly.

In mid-afternoon on Friday,
Newton saw the herd approaching

And rode out to meet it. Edwin
Said, "I somehow half expected
You to join us. Quit the army?"

"No," said Newton, "leave of absence."

III

Trailing up the Rio Grande,
They spent Sunday at Magoffin's
Ranch, a maverick was butchered,
Barbecued in earthen trenches,
And the drovers feasted, rested.

Two days later, at Fort Fillmore,
They bought seven barrels of flour,
Four new wagon wheels, some harness,
And a dozen other items
From the sutler. Major Backus
Wrote some letters introducing
Givens to the commandants at
Fort Thorn and Fort Yuma. Newton
Had known Backus at Fort Gibson.

Fifty miles and four days later
Givens entered in his journal:
"We have crossed the Rio Grande
And arrived at Fort Thorn. Major
Richardson said Quartermaster
Hays was in need of some cattle.
Post contractor, Milus Bennet,
Was delayed in his delivery
Of beef. Twenty head were needed.
We were glad to let him have them."

On another page the journal
Told about the trail they traveled:
"The topography of country
Bordering the Rio Grande
Is spectacular, distinctive;
Composition is of lofty
Mountains forested with scraggly
Evergreens and slashed by dizzy
Canyon walls carved by the ages . . .
In the distance, massive mesas
Blend into the haunting desert . . .
The most striking thing about it
To me is its sky at sunset
And at dawn. In all my travels
I have never known its equal:
World where lavender and blazing
Orange deck the sunset heavens
And where dawn is robed in yellows,
Pale greens, faint pinks, golds, and salmons
Known alone to these fantastic
Trails along the Rio Grande . . . "

IV

Drovers left Fort Thorn on Tuesday.
The Tanks and Mule Springs provided
Water for the oxen, horses
But not enough for the cattle.

When the herd reached *Rio Mimbres*
It was raining hard. The little
River swelled into a raging
Torrent. It was two days later

When the water had receded
To the point where they could ford it.

Pushing through a rugged region,
They passed *Ojo de la Vaca*
And Sycamore Creek, where water
Was sufficient for requirements.

Now they were again in mountain
Country and the herd was restless.
Bronco said that on his former
Trip the area was dry for
Sixty miles, but recent rainstorms
Had left pools of murky water
In ravines along the trailway.

V

Evening found the drovers camping
In the broken land approaching
Guadalupe Pass. Next morning
Cowboys goaded leery longhorns
Through about six miles of narrow
Boulder-strewn pass. It was roughest
By far of all trails encountered
Since they left the placid Clear Fork.

Wagons bringing up the rear were
Double-teamed, but still had trouble
Getting through the pass. The oxen
Leaned into their yokes and struggled
To negotiate the hazards
Of the steep and furrowed trailway.

In late afternoon encampment

Was made in a little valley
Just outside the pass. A gushing
Spring supplied them ample water.

It was evident that Indian
Scouts were watching every movement
As the cattle train crept onward.
Messages in smoke were relayed
Each day, and as night descended
Signal fires announced location
Of their camp, or told the watchers
That a night drive was in process.

VI

At the Springs San Bernardino
A rainstorm with rolling thunder
Caused a wild stampede. The longhorns
Ran for miles and scattered over
A wide area. The drovers
Spent three days in reassembling
Stock. The East San Pedro River
Was the next permanent water.
Grass was good along the river
Which they followed through the valley,
Letting livestock graze to regain
Strength and weight lost on the journey.

Two small wagon trains with trail herds
Were encamped on West San Pedro.

VII

Nearing Santa Cruz, some strangers
Rode into the camp at nightfall.

They reported that the Indians
Of the region were attacking
Wagon trains and stealing cattle.
On the twenty-first of August,
In an ambush in the mountains,
Indians sacked and burned the wagons
Of the Fairchild-McClure trail train,
Killed a member of the party,
Took the entire herd of cattle,
Numbering about two hundred.

Four days earlier the horse herd
Of the Dunlap train was raided
And most of the horses stolen.
Mrs. Dunlap's brother Houston
Was slain by the red marauders.
Next the Buck and Bryant trail train
Was attacked. A hundred forty
Cattle were lost in the foray.

Fourteen drovers led by Givens
Went with fifty other members
Of trail trains and Santa Cruzers
In search of the stolen livestock.

While returning to the camp site
From their fruitless search for raiders,
Givens and his men encountered
Some Apaches headed northward
With a herd of livestock stolen
From Mexican haciendas.
The Apaches, always eager
For a battle, started fighting,
Using antiquated rifles,

Bows and arrows, lances, war clubs.
They were no match for the well-armed
Drovers fighting under Givens.
When the short-lived fight was over,
Twelve Apache dead were counted,
While the others fled for cover.
Ninety animals were rounded
Up and added to the trail herd.

The drive westward was continued
Next day with no hint of Indians.

. . . Vegetation of the country
Ranged from chaparral and other
Shrubby growths to spreading thickets
Of mesquite and hardy badland
Plant life of a dozen species.

VIII

Pressing slowly toward the sunset,
Past a tame Apache village
And a tidy Pima mission,
On through mountains, desert stretches,
Drovers reached the town of Tucson
Where they bought supplies and rested
While repairs were made on wagons.

Timely rains and tiresome night drives
Saw the herd through arid regions
To a Gila River camp site.
For a week the stock was driven
Up the river toward the mountains . . ..
Dwindling bands of Mariposan
Red men, interspersed with Pimas,

Dwelled along the winding river.
Newton gave the squaws and chieftains
Gifts of kerchiefs, thread, and needles.

IX

On through mountain trails and deserts
Drovèrs urged the laggard cattle.
Drab dust devils danced and drifted
In the heat waves of the sandy
Wastes that stretched to bleak horizons . . .
Watching them in artless wonder
Young Mike Miller questioned Bronco:
"Is it true that Indian legend
Says dust devils are the evil
Spirits of departed tribesmen
Denied entrance to the Happy
Hunting Grounds and doomed to wander
Aimlessly across the desert?"

"Yes," said Bronco, "and tradition
Of the Mexicans who travel
Desert trails says that dust devils
Are the wraiths of early Spaniards
Lost when the *conquistadores*
Traveled arid wastes in search of
Precious stones and gold and silver.

"Superstitious Forty-Niners
Say they are the ghosts of miners
Killed for covetous claim-jumping.

"In reality, dust devils
Are lost souls of gone-wrong cowboys—
Hung or shot for cattle rustling . . . "

X

Past the Colorado River
Trudged the cattle train. The burning
Sand made night drives necessary.
Moonglow drenched the sandy wasteland
In a golden sheen of magic . . .
Newton's thoughts were of Lucinda
As he gazed in meditation
On the vastness spread before him:
"This land bears a sharp resemblance
To a great outdoor cathedral . . .
Dusky cloisters house a thousand
Icons sculptured by the patient
Winds of slowly marching ages . . .
Yucca candles, white and glowing,
Stand serene on hillside altars . . .
Thorned bouquets of blooming cacti
Grace the sand dunes piled haphazard
By the hand of time in passing."

Newton's musing was disrupted
By the sound of cattle plodding
Westward through the midnight desert.
Silver moonbeams danced a graceful
Quadrille ·on the long and gleaming
Horns, creating eerie shadows.
Joshua trees stood a lonely
Sentinel as riders prodded
Stragglers, keeping them from straying.
It was three A. M. and moondown
When they halted for a breather,
To await the early daybreak

Before pressing slowly onward.

XI

After passage through the desert,
Progress slowed as cattle fattened
On the fine nutritious grasses
Of rich California pastures.

Word had filtered through to gold towns
That a large herd of good Texas
Cattle neared the western market.
Representatives of merchant
Princes from a dozen gold camps
Met the herd at Warner's Meadow.
They bid eagerly for choicest
Cattle. In a single morning
The whole herd was sold at prices
That were pleasing to the owners.
Buyers paid with dusky nuggets,
Local medium of exchange.

At Los Angeles, Newton traded
Nuggets for gold coins. The drovers
Were paid off and many headed
For saloons and Spanish dance halls.

Saying farewell to the others,
After having made arrangements
With Bronco for the delivery
Of their mounts to Clear Fork Valley,
Newton and Edwin departed
For San Pedro. Then a steamer
Carried them to San Diego
Where a clipper ship was sailing
For New Orleans on the morrow.

Chapter Twenty-seven

Comanche Reservation

WAR DRUMS heralding the coming
Of Moscoso, Coronado,
And a host of other Spanish
Conquerors and colonizers
Were an overture to struggle
That was sealing fate of red men.

Through the lengthy span of Spanish
And Mexican domination
Of the spreading South Plains country,
The defense lines of its warriors
Kept the wild *Comancheria*
Intact and concealed its secrets.

By the middle Eighteen Fifties,
Three long centuries of warfare
Were approaching their denouement.
The fight to preserve ancestral
Domains from the avaricious
Dreams of growing streams of white men
Was too great for the defenders.

Destiny was contemplating
Final roles of the Comanche
Drama in the State of Texas.

True, the brave Comanche spirit
Would die slowly in the bosoms
Of the valiant Quanah Parker,
Para-a-coom, Mow-way, others,
But their fate was sealed and certain—
They would every one be banished
From the land that was their birthright.

II

Evil times beset the warriors;
White men pushed them ever westward.
Buffaloes were disappearing,
Clearly sand of time was dwindling
And the gay *Comancheria*
Smiled no longer. It was somber,
Like a man grown old and feeble,
Tottering toward life's last milestone.

Long the government had figured
Ways of dealing with the problems
That concerned the humanizing
Of the troublesome Comanches—
All experiments met failure.

Early as Eighteen Fifty-two,
Indian Agent Horace Capron
Visited the wasted village
Of Camanches on the Concho
And had found the Indians starving.

Said Katumse and Sanaco,
Rival chieftains of Comanches,
At a powwow held by Capron:
"To what can our tribes look forward?
Since we have no permanent home,
All our efforts toward crop raising
Have been thwarted by encroachment
Of the settlers ere our plantings
Could mature and we could harvest
Grain and crops to feed our people.

"In the olden day our fathers
Held possession undisputed
Of the vast *Comancheria*,
Free and happy were they always!
Now Comanches are but beggars!
Buffaloes, which were our larder,
And the other game we hunted,
Have been killed or driven thither
From the range that was our homeland.
We are forced into the sterile
Wastes with naught to stay our hunger.
We see but extermination:
We await with what forebearance
We can muster — it is meager.

"All we ask is some lone region
We can call our own to bury
Tribesmen without interference.

"Once a *padre* told the story
Of an evil man named Judas
Who, for thirty coins of silver,
Sold the Master of the Christians

To His enemies who took Him
To a high hill called Golgotha,
Nailed Him to a cross and killed Him
For naught save His benefactions.
We are like the white man's Jesus:
We have been betrayed through broken
Treaties made in solemn honor . . .
Robbed and beaten . . . Crucifixion
Would be merciful for red men."

The appeal of the Comanches,
While anathema to Texans,
Touched the hearts of some officials.

But the government was helpless;
For, on entering the Union,
Texas had reserved its public
Domain. The repeated efforts
Of officials who were in charge
Of affairs concerning Indians
Finally induced the Texas
Legislature to take action:
On the sixth of February,
Eigtheen Fifty-four, lawmakers
Set aside six leagues of public
Lands for Indian reservations.

III

Indian Agent Robert Neighbors,
Randolph Marcy, Colonel Lovelace
Headed searchers for land suited
For the granted reservations.
They examined barren badlands

Of the upper Colorado,
Wichita, and Brazos Rivers,
But found no sites for their purpose.

Realizing that the army
Would construct forts for protection
Of the Indian Reservations,
Lovelace told his old friend Marcy
That it might be advantageous
To reveal to Robert Neighbors
Virtues of the Clear Fork country.

"I had thought of that," said Marcy,
"But I was concerned how Newton
Might react to the idea."

"He would not object," said Lovelace."

"It would be ideally suited
As a home for the Comanches,"
Marcy reasoned, " and give Newton
The assurance that his ranching
Venture would be well protected."

"You are right," said Colonel Lovelace.
"I propose that on the morrow
We head for the Clear Fork Valley."

On the twentieth of August,
Where the Trail to California
Crosses little Qua-qua-ho-no*
Marcy, Lovelace and the agent
Called Comanches to a powwow.

"Father Washington has sent us,"

* Paint Creek

Said the spokesman for the trio,
"To establish reservations
For his worthy red-skinned children
Here within the Clear Fork Valley.

"Four Spanish leagues have been chosen
As a home for the Comanches.
Near confluence of the Clear Fork
And the Brazos, we selected
Other lands for the Andarkos,
Caddoes, Wacos, Tawakonis,
And the Tonkawas. Your future
Is secure if you will hearken
To the words of your White Father.
He will teach you cultivation
Of the soil and cattle raising.
Game, on which you have depended,
Soon will all be gone and shortly
You must learn another method
Of providing your requirements.
He will give you food and clothing
Until your first crops are ready
To be harvested and cattle
Have begun to show an increase.

IV

"In exchange for reservations
And the new life he will give you,
Father Washington demands that
You must cease your depredations.
If you do not, the White Father
Will send soldiers to destroy you."

Said Katumse and Sanaco,
Speaking for the braves and sub-chiefs,
"We remember what our former
Chieftain Mo-ko-cho-pe told us
Ere he died, and we endeavor
To comply with his last wishes:
After visiting Great Father
Washington, Chief Mo-ko-cho-pe
Brought his talk back to the prairies.
It was the same talk you give us
Now . . .'Tis good and we accept it.
We are glad that our White Father
Has remembered his red children.
We will accede to his wishes . . . "
Heads were nodded in approval.

"Now," the spokesman for the white men
Said, "we have gifts from White Father."
To the great delight of Indians,
They distributed the presents
That would seal the solemn compact.

There were kerchiefs, painted cottons,
Silver armlets, blankets, strouding,
Pans and knives and shawls and wampum.
These were treasures beyond wildest
Expectations of Comanches.

Next, a great feast was in order:
While the chiefs dined at head table,
Beeves were slaughtered for the other
Indians and they all made merry.

Lovelace had invited Marcy
To ride with him to the ranch site

Where they visited with Pilgrim.
From the well-stocked storehouse, Pilgrim
Sold them coffee, corn, and sugar
To complete the feast for Indians.

With full stomachs, the Comanches
Took a new look at the future.
Their bedazzled dreams and visions,
Taller than the tallest mountain
On the hazy blue horizon,
And as broad as sweeping prairies
Over which had roamed their fathers,
Were part of the dynanism
Of the reservation concept
In the minds of the Comanches . . .
They believed some stroke of magic
Would permit them to recapture
Halcyon days long since vanished
When Comanches were *The People*
And the prairies their possession . . .
They were doomed to disappointment.

Federal and state officials
Were elated with the outcome
Of the meeting with the Indians.
It was hoped the reservations
Would influence the solution
Of the complicated problems
That had kept the frontier regions
In a state of flux and turmoil.

If experiments succeeded
Other tribes might be encouraged

To give up nomadic customs
And submit to sedentary
Living on the reservation.

V

In September, Special Agent
G. H. Hill of the Comanches,
In reports to Robert Neighbors,
Now in charge of Texas Indians,
Stated that the Penetakas*
Were awaiting the fulfillment
Of the reservation promise
In anxiety and distress:
On one hand they were confronted
By advancement of the settlers;
On the other they were tempted
By their Yamparika** cousins
To resume their border-raiding . . .
Their situation was desperate.
Promised food was not forthcoming,
They were hungry and discouraged.

In November, Neighbors came from
San Antonio to check on
The Comanches. He was surprised
To find Chieftains Buffalo Hump,
Sanaco, and Katumse encamped
With a thousand of their tribesmen
On the river near Fort Belknap.

At a powwow chiefs insisted
That he hasten reservation

* Southern Comanches
** Northern Comanches

Preparations, as their people
Faced starvation. And they needed
A safe place to camp. The settlers
Had already reached Fort Belknap.

Neighbors told them he was ready
To keep promises he made them.
Plans were readied for the big move
To the Clear Fork Reservation.

VI

Based on half truth, speeding rumor
Flew to all but wreck the efforts
Toward successful reservations
Even while they were a-borning.

Back in Indian Territory,
While preparing for the journey
To locate the reservations,
Marcy had employed a Choctaw
Teamster to assist surveyors.
It was agreed that the Choctaw
Would be privileged to trade with
The Comanches as part payment
For his services. The Choctaw
Filled his wagon with prime trade goods:
Knives and calico, tobacco,
Ornamental beads, and wampum.
But he found on his arrival
In the valley of the Clear Fork
That impoverished conditions
Forbade trading at a profit.

The Comanches, fond of trading,
Told the Choctaw to be patient.
Soon they would have lots of horses
To exchange for his possessions.
Ere long border settlements were
Plagued with a new rash of raiding.
The Comanches kept their promise:
They returned with many horses
And much other loot for trading.
Before Neighbors left Fort Belknap,
Angry settlers came to plead with
Post Commander Major E. Steen
To assist them in recovery
Of their horses from Comanches.

Both Katumse and Sanaco
Volunteered to go with Major
Steen to all Comanche camp sites
Between Belknap and Fort Chadbourne
In search of the stolen horses.
As the searchers neared the Concho,
One of Chief Sanaco's warriors
Overtook him with a message
From a trusted German trader
That a large command of soldiers
Was en route to Clear Fork country
To annihilate Comanches.

Forthwith Chief Sanaco hastened
Back to his Comanche village
On the newborn reservation,
Sent forth runners to the other
Scattered bands along the Clear Fork;

Ere the sun had set that evening,
Buffalo Hump and Sanaco
Took their tribes and fled the country.
Nevermore would these two chieftains
Risk the safety of their people
On Comanche Reservation.

Chief Katumse placed no faith in
Rumors and convinced his tribesmen
That it was to their advantage
To stay on the reservation.

Captain Calhoun of Fort Chadbourne
Had been ordered out to search for
Raiding bands of Tanima and
Nakoni Comanches. Further,
He was told to attack any
Indians found along the border.

Acting Agent Hill and Neighbors
Censured Washington officials
Of the army for the mix-up
In orders which sorely threatened
The success of reservations.

In his report, Neighbors stated:
"This lack of cooperation
Is a typical example
Of the blunders that befoul us
In our efforts to civilize
The Comanches. Military
Personnel has no regard for
Problems of the personnel of
The Interior Department."

"Half a million dollars," Hill said,
"Could not restore calm conditions
That existed on the frontier
Forty days ago. The orders
Given Calhoun have imperiled
Our department's operation."

VIII

. . . Despite flight of most Comanches,
There were fewer than two hundred
On the Clear Fork Reservation,
Building plans proceeded smoothly.
Soon a dozen drop-log structures,
Homes for personnel and buildings
For supplies and tools and farming
Implements to teach Comanches
How to co-exist with white men
Rose in neat and prim precision
On the high bank of the Clear Fork.
The Comanches lived in teepees
Strewn across the reservation.

As surveyed, the reservation
Was comprised of a full township—
Six square miles of virgin landscape.
The topography was varied
From the broad and fertile valley
On the east side to the mountain
Brakes and canyons on the west side.

VIII

John R. Baylor, first official
Agent of the reservation,
Said, when he assumed his duties,
That the number of Comanches
Had grown to about three hundred.
"All of them are trouble-makers,
Wild and restless, discontented,"
Read the report he submitted
Shortly after his appointment.

Having but a small detachment
Of foot soldiers Baylor could not
Keep his charges, all well mounted,
In the reservation limits:
Indians rode at will on forays.
Baylor used conciliation
In his efforts to control them.
He was hopeful that the coming
Of the cavalry to Cooper
Would permit sufficient patrols
To halt raids upon the settlers.

Chapter Twenty-eight

Christmas In New Orleans

IT WAS CHRISTMAS Eve. The clipper
Ship was docking in New Orleans.

"It is good to be home," Edwin
Sighed as they walked down the gangplank.

Newton happily responded:
"Aye, just when I got my sea legs
Working and could taste the salty
Bite of sea wind and enjoy it,
The good fairy waves her wand and
I am changed to a landlubber."

Edwin looked at Newton sharply.
Newton smiled as Edwin ventured:
"I see you had the same feeling
I had," and his eyes were misty.

"The sea has a siren voice and
Both of us will always love it,"
Newton said as off they hurried
Toward home on Avenue St. Charles.

Christmas was a gay occasion.
The whole family was together;

Colonel Lovelace, on a furlough,
Had arrived in mid-December.
Uncle Jacque and Grand-Mere Dupuy
Had returned in late October
From the Natchez Trace plantation.

Lovelace mansion rang with gladsome
Greetings. There was merrymaking
Far across the Crescent City.
Balls and parties were attended
For a week. Then Colonel Lovelace
Said the time had come for parting.

II

"I have been assigned to study,"
Colonel Lovelace said to Newton,
"Frontier fort and troop conditions,
To determine a more rapid
Method of advancement westward.
Washington will be headquarters
While the survey is in progress.
I have asked for your assistance,
And my request has been granted."

Newton, Edwin, and the colonel
Left the third of January.
"I am having Edwin contact
A stone mason at Fort Belknap.
He can build the servant quarters
And get started on a second
Corral. He should have sufficient
Stone prepared to build the ranch house
By the time we reach the valley.

309

I'll return for you as soon as
This assignment is completed,"
Newton whispered to Lucinda
As he pressed her lips in parting.

"I'll be waiting," said Lucinda.

Givens and the colonel boarded
A boat for St. Louis, from where
They would go by stage and railroad
To Washington. Edwin started
His trip on an old stern-wheeler
Headed for Red River Landing,
Nearest port to Clear Fork Valley.

III

After an exhaustive study
Colonel Lovelace gave his report
To War Secretary Davis.

"With abandonment of Phantom,"
Read, in part, the detailed survey,
"Despite plans for reservations,
And a constant rash of raidings,
Texas troop count started falling
Well below its customary
Level. By Eighteen Fifty-four
Lands between the Colorado
And Red Rivers were defended
By four infantry companies
And two companies of dragoons,
These six companies were only
Skeletal in fabrication.

Lack of troops is universal,"
The report continued glumly,
"On the frontiers of the western
Advance toward Pacific Ocean.

"At a remote western outpost,
In the middle of the summer,
Indians ambushed young Lieutenant
John L. Grattan and his patrol.
Only one man had the fortune
To escape alive. He succumbed
To his wounds a short time later.

"Findings show eleven thousand
Officers and men are striving
To defend the lengthy frontier—
Some eight thousand miles extending—
Against forty thousand hostile
Braves of many Indian nations."

Davis used the information
To get congressional approval
For new regiments of soldiers,
Two of cavalry and two of
Infantry for frontier defense.

IV

Work in Washington completed,
Givens and the colonel started
Their return trip to the frontier.

At request of Colonel Lovelace
They had been assigned to duty
At Fort Belknap. They would select

A site on the reservation
For a post to house the soldiers
On their way to Clear Fork Valley
To insure that the Comanches
Were protected in the effort
Of the government to help them
Become civilized according
To the standards of the white man.

In a letter to Lucinda,
Newton carefully instructed
Her to take a boat to Shreveport,
And to wait for his arrival
At the home of distant cousins
On the Devereaux Plantation.
Shortly they would journey westward
To the ranch in Clear Fork Valley.
In a postscript Newton added:
"Darling, I am now a captain!"

V

Eighteen Fifty-five, In April,
Robert Edward Lee was ordered
To Kentucky to take charge of
A crack regiment, the Second
Cavalry, being assembled
In Louisville for a tour of
Duty on the Texas border.

Lee was serving in the absence
Of Commander Sidney Johnston.
Soon he transferred to Jefferson

Barracks, Missouri, to drill his
Men and season them for action.

Before orders came to transfer
The new regiment to Texas,
Lee received court martial duty,
And Second Cavalry command
Was returned to Colonel Johnston.
Colonel Lee would join them later.

VI

The regiment left Missouri
For the Clear Fork in October.
Down through Springfield and Neosho
Rode enthusiastic troopers.
Ozark Mountains were a dazzling
Burst of color and the soldiers
Gazed in raptured admiration
At the leaves of gold and russet
Shimmering in autumnal sunlight . . .
Blood-red sumac added glory
To the feast of fall's bright colors.

Early frosts had kissed persimmons
And the riders found them tasty.
Chinquapins were falling, bursting,
Spilling from their burry prisons;
Dragoons gathered them along with
Hazlenuts to spice their journey.

On through Indian Territory,
Via Tahlequah, Fort Gibson,
And Fort Washita, the troopers
Rode toward Texas frontier duty.

At the break of dawn the trumpets
Sounded "Boots and Saddles." Horsemen
Mounted merrily and started
Down the trail. A driving rainstorm
Failed to dampen ardent spirits.
Riders donned their gutta percha
Talmas and ignored the downpour.

On the fifteenth of December,
At the border town of Preston,
The contingent crossed Red River.

VII

The first night they spent in Texas
Was one to be long remembered.
Night camp fell in timbered country . . .
Icy rain beat down upon the
Smoke-filled tents and men had trouble
Staying warm. A stinging norther
Howled a banshee wail of Arctic
Cold descending upon Texas.

In the morning troops awakened
To a wonderland of beauty:
All the trees and branches sparkled
Like a host of diamonds dancing
In the glaring, dazzling sunlight.

Grasses gemmed with frosty crystals
Glistened brilliantly as sun rays
Bounced from one blade to another.

Noisy flights of prairie chickens
Flew from tree to tree or hovered
In rows on the ice-bound branches.

Troopers swore as horses skidded
Down the icy trail to Belknap.
Every step became a labor . . .
Moving forth across the prairie,
Distance stretched out more than ever . . .
Blue hills pointed out as landmarks
Seemed to move along before them.

At Fort Belknap they encountered
The severest winter weather
Known in many years in Texas.
Smoky tents were overcrowded
With the soldiers and civilians
Suffering from freezing weather.

A wagon train moving northward
From the Texas coast to meet them,
Lost more than a hundred oxen—
Frozen in sub-zero weather.

Nonetheless they celebrated
Christmas in a merry spirit.
Officers were served stout eggnog
And the quartermaster issued
Privates each a dram of whiskey.

VIII

Soon thereafter separation
Of the regiment was ordered.
Four outstanding companies went
To the Indian reservation

On the Clear Fork, where Camp Cooper
Was established. Newton joined them.
Freezing weather did not prevent
Balance of the men from marching
To Fort Mason. Distribution
Of the company by squadrons
Followed. Forts throughout the region
Were reenforced with mounted troops.
And, with cavalry on duty,
Efforts were resumed to subdue
Outlawed tribes of raiding red men.

Chapter Twenty-nine

Growing Pains

EIGHTEEN FIFTY-SIX, on April
Ninth, a gracious, seasoned soldier
Came to take command of Cooper,
Still a straggling, shapeless outpost
Where troops lived in tents and jacals
Until more substantial quarters,
Underway, could be completed.

Swift-winged scissortails and red birds
Added color to the peaceful
View that greeted the small wagon
Train that jounced down the uneven
Road that wound along the river.
Towering well above the lowland,
Like a lofty swinging garden,
Halfway up a lonely cliff side
Lay Camp Cooper lightly dozing
In the sun of early springtime.
When the wagon train was halted
At the camp, Lieutenant Colonel
Robert Edward Lee dismounted.
He had reached the post assigned him—

New commander of Camp Cooper.
On one side of the wide valley
Cliffs of chalky chrome and grayish
Limestone stood like battlemented
Castle walls of olden Scotland.
Prickly pear and chaparral grew
In luxuriant abandon,
As did springtime's first primroses
Midst the greening grama grasses.
Hackberry, elm, and pecan trees
Marked the winding Clear Fork River.
Antelope and deer and other
Wildlife ranged throughout the valley.

Stone Ranch was alive with builders
Striving to complete construction.
Nearby, workmen were engaged in
Taking limestone from a quarry.

Inconspicuously the teepees,
Reminiscent of the ancient
Panoply of free Comanches,
Stood in contrast to the modern
Camp, ranch, reservation buildings
Going up throughout the valley.
Well beyond the scene of action
Grazed the Givens' herds of livestock.

II

Robert Lee and Newton Givens
Had met often on the battle
Fields of Mexico — Jalapa,
Contreras and Churubusco.

When they first met at Camp Cooper,
They spent many hours of pleasant
Reminiscing and re-living
Days they knew south of the border.

At the ranch, Lee met Lucinda
And the children. They reminded
Him of Arlington and Mary
And his own beloved family.

"When the ranch house is completed,"
Newton told his guest, "I want you
To join me in panther hunting."

"It will be my pleasure," Lee said.

III

One spring morning, Agent Baylor
Called the Indians into council.
"It is time," he said, "for planting.
I have hired an expert farmer,
And day laborers have broken
Something like a hundred acres
Of rich botton land for truck crops
And for grain to feed your livestock."

Pleased, Katumse and his warriors
Planted vegetables and grain crops.
Long and hard Comanches labored
In the fields along the Clear Fork.
In the evening, tired and weary,
They would return to their teepees.
The enchanting hour of twilight,
Canopied in ghost-clouds sailing

Through a sea of tinted moon mist,
Lulled their cares and dancers gathered
To petition gods of planting
To be merciful and send them
Harvest laden with abundance
That their women and their children
Might no longer have to suffer
From the gnawing pangs of hunger.

IV

Crops grew rapidly and prospects
Were so good that Chief Katumse's
Hungry kinsmen on the prairies
Heard about them and descended
On the reservation in such
Numbers that the population
Doubled. There were now six hundred.

Then the prospects turned to ashes:
Rains ceased and the crops stopped growing.
Rain gods did not hear their pleadings . . .
If they did, they did not answer.
It is true that flashing lightning
Lighted heavens; rolling thunder
Echoed through the far-off mesas;
But each new day dawned on dryer
Land than did the day preceding.
Hills were mantled in the somber
Robes of dust that left their patches
Of corn, peas, beans, pumpkins, melons
Dying under scorching heat waves.

One hot morning, Indians gazing
Toward the north saw heaven darken
As grasshoppers by the millions
Poured into their fields and patches—
When they passed, the earth was barren.

Now the superstitious Indians
Were convinced the gods were angry
With them for having abandoned
Former ways to follow white men . . .

But the government insisted
It would stand by its agreement—
Food and clothes would be forthcoming.

"We will stay," said the Comanches.

V

Gradually the dark clouds rifted
Over changing Clear Fork Valley
And a rainbow graced the shoulders
Of the hills and staggered mesas.

Nondescript, makeshift, and flimsy
Tarpaulin and tented shelters
Of Camp Cooper were transmuted
Into structures that suggested
Permanence. The military
Bearing of the post befitted
Its position of importance
On the frontier of West Texas.

Narrow trails were growing wider
To support increasing traffic.
Sharp commands upon the drill field

Bespoke soldiers being fitted
For the big job of assisting
In expansion of the region.

VI

The Comanche Reservation
For the moment held high promise
Of fulfilling its intended
Mission as prescribed by Neighbors
And officials of Department
Of Interior and Indians.

People far across the nation
Eyed experiments in hopeful
Eagerness that the Comanche
Could be civilized and aided
In becoming a productive
Member of the social system.

VII

Five miles down the winding trailway
Stone Ranch carpenters and masons
Watched the rock and lumber blossom
Into Newton and Lucinda's
Dream house · — first of all constructed
In the virgin land, West Texas.

Frontier houses as a rule were
Little more than shabby shelters
Made of pickets standing upright
In the earth. Wide cracks were chinked with
Mortar, mud, clay, or adobe.
Doors were clap board hung on wooden
Hinges, or a strip of rawhide.

Chimneys were a combination
Of sticks and dirt, rocks and mortar.
Windows were unknown, and homemade
Furniture was crude and added
Little comfort for the household.

By comparison the Givens
Ranch plant was a rare oasis
In a land that swayed and wavered
Between savagery and promise
Of a plucky rancher's Eden.

The main house grew like a fortress,
Calculated to withstand the
Ravages of time, the ceaseless
Toll of elements' exaction.
It consisted of two large rooms,
Each about sixteen by twenty;
Twelve feet wide, a stately hallway,
Closed by double doors at each end,
Formed a third room, twelve by twenty.

Doors and window sashes, shingles,
Hardware, and the other items
Necessary for the structure
Were hauled from San Antonio,
Some three hundred miles to southward,
By ox wagons through a country
Teeming with marauding Indians.

From the hallway, which in summer
Could be opened for a breezeway,
Heavy single oak doors opened
Into the other compartments.

On each side of the larger rooms
Spacious windows looked out upon
Scenes of sheer primeval beauty.

Floors of one room and the hallway
Were of smoothest limestone flagging,
While the other room was boastful
Of a wooden floor for added
Comfort and a fond reminder
Of refinements in the city
They had left behind in casting
Lots upon the wildest border
That in all the States existed . . .

Massive doors were crowned with transoms,
And the rooms were light and airy.
High, thick walls invited coolness
During the hot days of summer.
Winter warmth was well provided
By fireplaces — huge, attractive,
With precision-sculptured mantels.
Finishing throughout the building
Was complete in minute detail.

Kitchen, dining room, and quarters
For the servants were located
In a smaller building near the
Northwest corner of the main house.
Workmanship in this house also
Was a testament to Newton's
Taste for durability and
Comfort, better living, beauty.
There were two rooms in the building

With a chimney in the center
And a cozy fireplace opening
Into each room spilling cheery
Comfort through the days of winter
When the howling, stinging northers
Swooped across the distant mesas.

On the southern side of gentle
Walnut Creek, a cool spring tumbled
Sparkling waters from the bosom
Of the earth. Another stone house,
Bearing out the sturdy motif,
Was erected for protection
Of the clear, refreshing fountain
Gurgling from the ground to furnish
Drinking water for the household.
Too, it was refrigeration
By a kindly nature given
To preserve the milk and butter
And fresh meat throughout the summer
And the warmer days of autumn.

The smokehouse was situated
West of the main house and kitchen.
Built to generous proportions,
It would hold an ample supply
Of fine meats for all occasions.
In addition to the wild game,
Of which there was an abundance,
There was beef and pork and mutton.

When the ranch plant was completed
Edwin was sent to Kentucky
To buy thoroughbreds to be used
As mounts for the chase, and racing.

Thus the first West Texas venture
In the fascinating record
Of the storied realm of ranching
Grew apace in Clear Fork Valley.

VIII

In his hunts for mountain lions,
Panthers, antelope, and lobos,
Givens won the reputation
Of a Nimrod without equal
On the whole frontier of Texas.
With his pack of some three dozen
Blooded hunting hounds he featured
A bull terrier named *Fearless*—
"Teaches courage to the others,"
Smiled the captain to his cronies.

IX

More and more the rolling ranges,
Rivers, mountains, bleak escarpments
Grew on Givens. The impression
That they made upon his conscience
Led to new appreciation
Of the finer things existing
In the hearts of pioneering
Men and women on the frontiers
Of life's endless explorations.

Gradually he grew more rugged
Than the land he sought to conquer.
The viccisitudes of nature—

Floods and droughts and freezing northers,
Sand storms, twisters, blazing heat waves—
All conspiring to sudbue him,
Only served to make him stronger
In the realm of spirit, patience,
Tolerance and understanding.

Metamorphosis came slowly,
But it was pronounced and certain.
Those who witnessed it respected
Him and stood in awe and wonder
At his dignity and prudence.

There was no way to establish
A relationship familiar;
This he reserved for his family.
Yet each knew that he could carry
Any burden to the captain
Whose sage advice and gentle counsel
Could be counted on in solving
Problems of whatever nature.

From a twilight zone of mystery
He emerged transformed and brimming
With eternal optimism,
Stamina, and perseverance.
Thus evolved the nobler aspects
And the enterprising spirit
Of that special breed of mankind
Destined to become The Texan—
Legacy of Newton Givens
Who was first to claim the challenge
Of the elements that forged him
Into a West Texas rancher.

Chapter Thirty

Life at the Ranch

WHEN SPRING faded into summer,
In the stillness of the evening,
Arm in arm the happy couple
Strolled, enraptured, near the springhouse.

"Listen," Newton whispered softly,
"To the love song of the water,
Telling how much I adore you!
Dear, my love is no less constant
Than the ever-flowing springlet."

"You too listen, Newton Givens,"
Came the carefree, glad rejoinder,
"To the breezes softly singing
In the interlocking branches
Of the overspreading elm trees:
Hear them say, 'My one and only
True love, I shall always cherish
You and thank the gods for sending
You my way to be my husband'."

As the sunset changed from glowing
Red and pink to dusky purple,
Sounds of nighttime from the distance
Blended in melodic cadence
With the symphony of soothing
Vespers offered by the twilight.
These were moments of fulfillment
Of their love so deep and tender
That it left them spent and breathless—
When they knew the perfect oneness
Of their spirits with their maker's—
Love that passeth understanding . . .

II

The Clear Fork was late-fall dozing.
Not a minnow played the riffle
At the ford. A few fat turkeys
Fed in underbrush. The birds sang
Doleful songs that marked the naked
Timber basking in the sunlight.
Fallish squalls were storing water
In the flat tanks in the lowlands:
Frost lay heavy on the rushes
In the thin ice near the edges.
Teals and mallards fed and rested
Farther out in open water.

"Time to kill the hogs and butcher,"
Pilgrim said on Tuesday morning.

David set the scalding barrel,
Hung the hoisting ropes and pulleys,
And arranged the rough-board tables.

329

Fires were blazing, water boiling,
And the hogs, as if they harbored
Some uncanny premonition
Of impending doom, squealed shrilly.

Butchering time entailed firing
Up the smokehouse, making sausage,
Hogshead cheese, and pickling pigs' feet;
Boiling backbone, frying sweetbread,
Fixing chitterlings and scrapple;
Rendering lard, pressing cracklings,
Smoking hams and slabs of bacon.

It was also time for making
Soap and hominy. Conchita
Scrubbed the barrels, tubs, and kettles
Till they sparkled. All was ready.
And the next ten days were busy,
Happy times — with much good eating.

III

Stone Ranch was the epitome
Of frontier hospitality:
The Givenses were perfect hosts,
As gracious as their friendly toasts
Were warming to the rich or poor
Who chanced to knock upon their door.
All passers-by were welcomed here,
Admitted to the gladsome cheer
That permeated every room,
Dispelling all the chill and gloom

Of those who often rode with fear
The lonely trails of the frontier.

IV

On many chilling winter nights,
When northers howled in gusty flights,
The Givens household gathered round
The huge fireplace, and joyful sound
Rang out as voices, gay and clear,
Sang songs that to their hearts were dear.
Full many winter tales were told
Of other lands and pirates bold.

Lucinda told, with Southern grace,
Of life along the Natchez Trace.
The captain would respond with tales
Of England and the Prince of Wales;
Of the lands he had wandered through
From Halifax to Timbuktu.
Sometimes Conchita or Ramon,
Whom they had brought from San Antone
To do the cooking and the chores
Within the house and out-of-doors,
Would strum the zither and would sing
Their haunting Spanish songs of spring
And love beside the Alamo
When it belonged to Mexico.

When guileless, sleepy prayers were said,
While children knelt by trundle bed,
And their lingering good-night kiss
Was planted mid the joy and bliss

That spread around the simple scene
Like a protective angel-screen,
Lucinda, filled with love and pride,
Sat happily at Newton's side:
They watched the flames leap crazily
And meditated lazily
Upon the why of life and how
Their love had blossomed until now . . .
It seemed that there could never be
Another love so full and free!

V

They dreamed the dreams that all men know
When life and love are full aglow:
A life of sound prosperity
Was meant for them; posterity
Would carry on when came the day
That they should stow their joys away
Upon the chariot of time
And journey to that land sublime
Where love spans all adversity
And blends into eternity.

Although it was a lonely life
In some respects, and tinged with strife,
The greater part of it was gay,
For love was king, and joy held sway.
They worshipped God and gave Him praise
For all the wondrous happy days.

. . . How merciful that God conceals
From man the awful woe that steals

The sunshine from the brightest day
And plunges man into a way
Where he must grope and fight for breath,
And sometimes even pray for death
To come and give him swift relief
From heartache, pain, and stifling grief!

VI

Skillful architect was Givens,
Man of intellect and vision,
Man of pioneering spirit,
Worthy of the tribute due him
As adventurous forerunner
Of the ranchmen of West Texas.

His keen knowledge of the basic
Principles of gainful ranching
Was apparent in his every
Studied, well-directed action.
Dreams he nurtured failed fruition
By the hapless intervention
Of the fate that leads men onward
To success or dismal failure . . .

VII

His achievement in erection
Of the comprehensive ranch plant
And the brief time that he lived there
Were his meager compensation.
Meager? Or was it a lavish
Benediction, sheer and subtle,

333

Known to those few who are chosen
To perform some lofty service
In a field of high endeavor
For their toiling, burdened brothers?

When a man has scaled the topmost
Peak that others cannot conquer
Due to hazards of the journey,
Who can tell him, "Nay, 'tis not so,"
When he recounts mighty marvels
He has witnessed from the summit?

VIII

Gnarled mesquite trees gently swaying
In the soothing breeze of autumn,
Hum a solemn dirge of mourning
For the fleeting thread of glory,
In the warp and woof fantastic,
Weaving in and out the pattern
Of Stone Ranch's tragic story . . .

While his vision of an estate
Carved from out the rolling expanse
Of the lush and wild frontierland
Was foredoomed to dissolution
In the crucible of whimsic
Destiny bereft of reason,
Certainly he left a model
For the ranchers of the region
Soon to follow in his footsteps.

IX

He it was who dropped the gauntlet,
Hurled the challenge keen and heady
To that dauntless breed of Texans
Who would come to claim and conquer
This fair land of restless grandeur.

. . . Where he failed through circumstances
Mapped by destiny to snare him,
They would win the golden trophy
Of the Clear Fork Valley ranch lands.

They would become part and parcel
Of the stirring rough-hewn saga
Of the Old West and traditions
That would pass on to their children
In ensuing generations.

They would see the disappearance
In a few short years of struggle
Of the savage, brutish outlands,
And their permanent replacement
With refinement, law, and order.

Chapter Thirty-one

Mounting Tension

EIGHTEEN FIFTY-EIGHT, in August,
Santa Anna, a Comanche
With unsavory reputation,
And companion, a Nokoni
Warrior, bent on stealing horses
From the settlers to the eastward,
Visited the reservation.

They refused Katumse's orders
To depart. When Agent Leeper
Was informed of their decision
To remain, he sent to Cooper
For Lieutenant Van Camp to bring
Troopers to expel the outlaws.

There were only nineteen soldiers
At the post, the others being
Out on various assignments.

The excited Indians, watching
The approach of mounted troopers,
Jumped to the inept conclusion
That the soldiers meant to slay them.

Ignoring pleas of Katumse,
A large mob of angry warriors
Armed with rifles, bows, and arrows,
Threatened to attack the troopers
Unless there was a withdrawal.

Van Camp, unimpressed, gave orders
For his men to search the teepee
Where the renegades were hiding.
This enraged the warriors further.
They were deaf to Chief Katumse's
Pleas for a return to order.

Sub-Chief Tosh-e-weh, a spokesman
For the rebels, said that every
Brave in his group stood full ready
To die rather than see their guests
Expelled by the Cooper soldiers.

Chief Katumse then sprang forward
In an effort to deliver
The visitors to the soldiers.
Thirty-odd squaws barred the chieftain's
Entry to the teepee, pleading
With him to cause no more trouble.

II

Halted by the Squaws, Katumse
Asked that all loyal Comanches
Stand beside him, Van Camp, Leeper:
Only five Indians responded.
To add to other confusion
The sergeant in charge told Van Camp

337

That one round of ammunition
Was all that troopers had with them—
And there was no more at Cooper!

Van Camp was nonplussed. Around him
And his sore imperiled troopers
Raged the angry, shouting Indians.
With no other course to follow,
Van Camp ordered a withdrawal.

III

Late that afternoon Tosh-e-weh,
Heading fifty choice Comanches,
Called on Leeper, bent on murder.

Leeper, sensing their intention,
Talked with grim determination
And persuaded Tosh-e-weh to
Reconsider plans and spare him.

In a calm powwow that followed,
Tosh-e-weh revealed that hostile
Threats made earlier resulted
From a rumor that the soldiers
Had come to the reservation
To annihilate the Indians.

Tosh-e-weh accepted Leeper's
Word that he and Van Camp wanted
Only to assist Comanches.
Leeper granted him permission
To escort the outlaw red men
From the reserve with assurance
That they would not be molested.

338

IV

News of Tosh-e-weh's protection
Of the horse thieves reached the outmost
Camp of Indians and encouraged
Them to make the reservation
Haven for marauding parties.

Many times the angered settlers
Followed trails to the Comanche
Reservation, and their horses
Usually were found included
In the horse herds of the Indians.

Chief Katumse stoutly maintained
That neither he nor his people
Were responsible for horse theft—
That it was the work of wild tribes.

When Katumse's braves were threatened
With violence for livestock stealing,
Military and civilian
Law enforcers asked for concrete
Evidence to back the charges.
This could not be furnished. Settlers
Claimed that federal officials
Were condoning and abetting
Thievery and border raiding.
Inability to settle
Matters on deliberative
Levels naturally resulted
In confusion and vexation.

Rapidly conditions worsened
Until the frontier of Texas
Was a tinderbox of trouble.

V

On the fifth day of December,
An armed force of self-appointed
"Rangers" fell at night upon a
Sleeping camp of unsuspecting
Indians, killing seven of them.
They were Caddoes and Andarkos,
Led by Choctaw Tom, respected
Brazos Reservation leader,
Who with knowledge of their agent
Had gone hunting. Some had returned
To the reserve, ponies laden
With wild game, but others lingered
At some settlers' invitation
To go with them on a bear hunt.

The authorities at Cooper
And both Indian reservations
Bitterly denounced the wanton
Massacre of friendly red men.

In a special proclamation,
Runnels, Governor of Texas,
Ordered the arrest of "rangers,"
But they never were indicted.
Most grand juries were allergic

To indicting any white man
Charged with crime against the Indians.

VI

There was an extant fixation
That the reservation Indians
Were responsible for high crimes
Perpetrated by the wild tribes.

Those who lived near reservations
Knew the Indians to be friendly
And dependable. The agents,
Ross and Leeper, were courageous
Men attempting to bring order
Out of chaos. Under Neighbors
They worked hard at educating
Charges in the ways of white men,
Guiding them with gentle patience
And protecting them with valor.
Following the Choctaw Tom raid,
Frontier sentiment reacted
In a strange, ironic manner:
Robert Neighbors talked the Indians
Out of a retalitory
Engagement, but the white aggressors,
Strongly fearing a reprisal,
Started campaigns for removal
Of the reservation red men
To the Indian Territory.

VII

Growing border Indian furor
Fanned the tensions that were rending
North and South. A new voice sounded
Out in ceaseless agitation:
John R. Baylor long had harbored
Personal grievances resulting
From his summary dismissal
As head of the reservation.

The irascible, contentious
Baylor also was persuasive
And had little trouble finding
Followers among disgruntled
Settlers who would go to any
Length to rid themselves of Indians.

Chapter Thirty-two

Reservation War

BLUSTERY WINDS of March were blowing
When a weary patrol wended
Its way up the Clear Fork Valley
To Camp Cooper. Slowly Newton,
Head of the patrol, dismounted,
Wrote out his report, and headed
For the ranch. Lucinda greeted
Him with warmth. "You look so weary,
Newton, darling. What has happened?"

"I'm discouraged," Newton answered.
"It appears that all the labor
Poured into the reservations
May have gone for naught. John Baylor
Has declared war on all Indians
And both of the reservations."

"How can this be?" asked Lucinda.
"Surely governmental forces
Will forestall such reckless action."

"Wasn't Baylor once invited
On a panther hunt you sponsored

For some officers at Cooper?"
Edwin asked and Newton nodded.

"Yes, when I first met the fellow,
He was the Comanche agent.
And, you know, I took a fancy
To the man. He seemed quite friendly.
He was interesting. His background,
Actually, is most impressive.
His grandfather, great-grandfather,
And three great-uncles saw service
Under Washington in days of
American Revolution.
And his father, Dr. Baylor,
Was physician at Fort Gibson.

"John R. moved on down to Texas,
Read law, and was soon elected
To the Texas Legislature.
He could just not seem to fit in
Any governmental picture,
Discipline was foreign to him.
He must have been born a rebel.
There are some men who seem destined
To precipitate the people
Into bloody strife and turmoil.

"He became an Indian-hater
When he lost his job as agent.
He is bitter and vindictive
But has power to sway hot-blooded
Men, and there are many settlers
Who will follow where he leads them.

"Last week at Rock Creek he ordered
An assembly of frontiersmen
For the purpose of attacking
Reservations. The Comanches
Were considered worst offenders,
But the Brazos Reservation,
Being nearer settlements and
A much stronger Indian center,
Was placed first on his agenda.

"Word leaked out that Captain John King,
With a company of soldiers,
Had been sent in for protection
Of the Indians, who themselves were
Barricaded, armed, and ready
To defend the reservation.
This disheartened Baylor's army.
Plans to attack were abandoned.

"But John Baylor is no quitter.
He will strike again. Much harder!"

II

Newton, coughing, roused Lucinda
From her early morning slumber.
"Have you caught a cold, my darling?"
Anxiously Lucinda questioned.

"No, I think not," answered Newton.
"I am not sure what's the matter . . .
It was just a spell of coughing;
I will be all right directly."

At the breakfast table, Newton
Said that he was feeling puny.
"I will drive you to Camp Cooper,"
Said Lucinda, "to the doctor."

"No, I'm just tired," Newton answered.
"I will be fine by tomorrow."

Later in the day Lucinda
Said, "Let's take a walk," and Newton
Answered, "Yes, a stroll might help me."

Soft sweet-smelling April floated
Gently over Clear Fork Valley.
Redbirds, bluebirds, wrens, and robbins
Twittered melodies of springtime.

The plum thicket, white with fluffy
Blossoms, hosted swarms of humming
Bees and served them rich sweet pollen.
Butterflies of varied colors
Skimmed across the snow-white bloomage,
Pleasuring themselves in sunshine.

Breezes playing by the streamlet
Hummed in low tones to the flowers.
And the smoothly flowing water
Clucked to rocks along the riffles.

"I feel better, sweetheart," Newton
Said. "A walk was all I needed."

"No," Lucinda answered, "something
Is wrong. You have dark half circles
Underneath your eyes. That coughing
Paroxysm has me worried."

"You're too beautiful to worry,"
Bantered Newton. "You're as pretty
As the day — and it is perfect!"

As they walked back toward the ranch house,
They kept up a lively chatter,
Trying to conceal the secret
Twinge that bordered on foreboding
Each felt in his inner being.

III

Adding fuel to the flaring
Flames of frenzy that were gnawing
At the heart of all the region,
Members of the self-styled rangers
Killed a well-known Indian runner
Employed as a message bearer
For the U. S. troops who guarded
Brazos Indian Reservation.

When the courier, expected
At the reserve, did not show up,
Young Lieutenant William Burnet,
Fearing that the worst had happened,
Formed a searching party composed
Of the reservation farmer,
Two soldiers, and some one hundred
Well-armed reservation warriors,
And set out to hunt the runner.

En route to Jacksboro he learned
That a fifteen-member party
Of Jack County rangers, searching

For Indians, had killed the runner. ·
When he found the mutilated
And scalped body, the lieutenant
Vowed to follow and to punish
"Those murderers and mail robbers,"
As he called them in a letter
Written later to his father,
Former president of Texas.

William Burnet led his warriors
Into Jacksboro in search of
Those responsible for killing
The messenger but he did not
Find them. They had been well hidden.

His search of the town resulted '
In a rash of scathing rumors
That grew wilder as they traveled:
"Jacksboro has been invaded,"
Screamed the rumors, "by the Indians
Seeking revenge for the death of
Their murderous fellow tribesman!"

IV

"Now the time has come for action!"
Ran the Baylor propaganda,
"All the Indians must be slaughtered,
Or be driven from the country!"

The "Frontier Army of Defense"
Sprang to life with the intention
Of "erasing reservations."

May, the twenty-third, John Baylor
Led his army of three hundred
Men against the Brazos Reserve.

Captain J. B. Plummer, serving
As commander of the soldiers
On guard at the reservation,
Talked with Baylor and was informed
That his army came "to assail
Indians of the reservation
But not to attack the white men."

Plummer answered that "the troopers
Are here to protect the Indians . . .
They will surely do their duty."

Baylor quailed and called a retreat.
As his army left, an Indian
Was killed, and the other warriors
Followed and attacked invaders,
Killing three and wounding others.

Baylor sought aid for his wounded
Men at Belknap village, but his
Army got a cold reception.

As frontier excitement crested,
Baylor sent word to settlements,
Calling for "a thousand rangers
To attack the reservation
And the soldiers there to guard them.

Volunteers were asked to gather
At Rock Creek from whence they would march
On both of the reservations.

Major Van Dorn, ran strong rumor,
Was prepared to stop invaders.
Five full companies of soldiers,
Many of them from Camp Cooper,
Were coming as reinforcements
To the garrison at Brazos.
The Frontier Army of Defense
Heard the rumor and believed it.

It was Thursday, June the second,
When a mutiny erupted
That could not be quelled by Baylor.
When the bubble burst, his army
Melted and the war was ended.
But the cause of reservations
. Had been lost. The din and clamor
Had been heard, and reservations
Shortly were to be abandoned.

V

. . . On the thirty-first of July,
Under guard of Captain Gilbert
And a company of troopers,
A bedraggled cavalcade of
Two-wheeled Mexican *carretas*,
Travois, ambulances, wagons,
And the downcast, whipped Comanches,
Lugging pitiful possessions,
Plodded down the reservation
Road that beckoned toward Red River.

Newton and Lucinda, watching,
Sighed as sad-faced Matthew Leeper

Led his charges from the valley
Into a decadent exile.

"They were not to blame, Lucinda
Said "for rapine, pillage, murder
Charged to them by wanton white men."

. . . At Steen Crossing on Red River,
Lion-hearted Robert Neighbors,
Gaunt, dejected, and despondent,
With his weary, hungry charges
From the Brazos Reservation,
Under guard of George H. Thomas,
Joined the cavalcade. Together
Toward oblivion they struggled.
Thus the curtain fell on efforts
To civilize the Comanches.

VI

. . . An assassin's bullet ended
Robert Neighbor's life at Belknap
On the thirteenth of September.
On his return trip to Texas
From the Indian Territory,
Neighbors spent the night at Belknap.
In the morning as he started
Over to another building
To confer with Matthew Leeper,
A man by the name of Cornett
Shot him with a double-barrel
Shotgun because "He was too good
To that sorry scum, the red skins!"

Chapter Thirty-three

The Overland Mail

ON A MILD DAY in December
Little Newton rode with Bitsy
Past the cattle herd and onward
Toward the limpid Clear Fork River.

"This is stage day," Little Newton
Said. "How would you like to see it?"

Bitsy thought a moment, answered:
"I would like it fine, but Mamma
Says we are not to ride farther
Than the sheepfold where the shepherd
Can keep us in view, remember?"

"Aw," he answered, "she won't know it.
Come on. Simon will not see us.
I go there when I get ready.
When the stage conductor sees me,
He waves. Once he blew his bugle,
And the passengers and driver
All saw me, and everyone waved."

"Well," said Bitsy, if you're certain
It will be all right . . . I guess so."

Off they loped. Their eager ponies
Soon arrived at a small hilltop
Just above the road. The children
Had not long to wait. A rumble
Sounded and a dust cloud circled.

II

"Here she comes," cried Little Newton,
"Right on time, or maybe early!"

Six Missouri mules galloped
At a speed that frightened Bitsy.
And the huge coach careened madly
As the driver popped his long whip.

"Wave!" cried Little Newton loudly.
"Wave and holler! They don't see us!"

Just then the conductor spotted
The children and blew his stage horn.
Passengers glanced out and saw them,
And returned the frenzied greeting.
As the coach was disappearing
Round a bend and dust was settling,
Edwin rode up, feigning anger
At discovering the children
So far from their prescribed limits.

Many explanations followed
As they rode back toward the ranch house.
Little Newton took the blame and
Promised faithfully to never
Again go beyond the sheepcote
If Edwin would not tell Newton
Of their escapade. He promised.

That night by the cozy fireside,
Little Newton told his father:
"I would like to hear the story
Of how the stage line was started."

"Yes," joined Bitsy, "Daddy, tell us!"

III

"Well," said Newton, "it's a story
Of accomplishment in travel
And mail service to the nation
That beggars imagination.
Men still wonder how it was done!
"I suppose the story started
Many years ago in Congress.
Forty-niners, who by thousands
Made their way to California,
Joined by Salt Lake City Mormons,
Cried for mail from home. A contract
Was awarded, Eighteen Fifty,
By the Post Office Department,
For a mail route from Missouri
To Salt Lake in distant Utah.
The next year another contract
Was let to continue service
To Placerville, California.

"This was the start of a series
Of mail routes to the Pacific.
Countless hazards, weather, mountains,
Deserts, politics, and Indians
Posed their threats from the beginning
To success of early mail routes.

"For a time a bold Norwegian,
Snowshoe Thompson, carried the mail
On foot through the high Sierras.

IV

"But political chicanery
Was the greatest of all problems.
War between the states was looming
Even then, just as it still is.
Both the North and South were plotting
To control the western gold fields
When, and if, the war is started.

"A. V. Brown, postmaster general,
Was a Southerner. When Congress
Last year passed legislation
Authorizing a through mail line
From the Mississippi River
To San Francisco, he selected
A route so far south it entered
Mexico before it ended.

"Contract terms were toughest ever
Devised. Semi-weekly service
Over the twenty-eight-hundred-
Mile route had to be completed
In the span of forty-five days.

"Such speed was beyond the realm of
Average imagination.
'It cannot be done,' said people.
The line must be operating
In one year from date of contract.

"The contract provided payment
Of six hundred thousand dollars
Annually in addition
To the fares paid by passengers.

V

"While newspapers, politicians,
And the public hotly argued
That the job could not be mastered,
One man eagerly insisted
That it could. He was preparing
To accept the mammoth challenge.

"Without doubt, the most outstanding
Stagecoach man in all the country
Was John Butterfield, a wealthy
New York transportation magnate.

"Butterfield investigated
Every phase of the tremendous
Undertaking, placed his bid, and
Finally it was accepted.

"He organized a two million
Dollar company and started
Men to working on all aspects
Of the project. Engineers were
Hired to lay out roads where only
Trails had previously existed.

"Magnitude of preparations
Surpassed all preceding efforts
In the field of transportation.

"He immediately ordered
Two hundred fifty stagecoaches,
Scores of wagons, prairie schooners,
Several hundred sets of harness,
Stage horns, horseshoe nails, and horseshoes,
Entire blacksmith shop equipment,
Tank wagons for hauling water
To stations in desert country,
And two thousand head of horses.
He sent scouts across the country
Searching for the best stage drivers.

"In a year of preparation,
Building roads and bridges, stations,
Storing hay and grain for horses,
Working hundreds of men from each
End of the line, John Butterfield
Spent more than a million dollars.
But when time came, he was ready
To begin the operation.

VI

"On the sixteenth of September
At the rail-head town of Tipton,
In Missouri, a new stagecoach,
Brightly painted, hitched to six of
Finest horses from the stables
Of the Southern Overland Mail
Waited at the railroad station.

"At seven o'clock that evening
Young John Butterfield was stationed

On the driver's seat. His father
And six passengers were seated
In the stagecoach. At a signal
From his father, Young John started
The first trip to California.

"Seven miles from Tipton was the
First station, and twenty minutes
Was allowed for changing horses
And to eat a hot meal prepared
By the wife of station agent.

"In the settled eastern country
Twenty miles was farthest distance
Between stations. A coaching horn
Was blown to warn the keeper
To have horses and food ready:
Not a moment could be lost if
Coaches were to keep their schedules.

VII

"At two o'clock in the morning
Of the nineteenth of September,
The first westbound stagecoach entered
Fort Smith where a celebration
Was in progress, paying tribute
To the newly founded stage line—
The connecting link between the
East and West, a link long needed
In realms of communication.

"Fort Smith was the destination
Of the Butterfields and other

Passengers with one exception:
A young writer for *The New York
Herald*, Waterman L. Ormsby,
Was assigned to record the trip
All the way to California.

"In spite of the celebration
In Fort Smith, the stagecoach hurried
On as soon as hostlers exchanged
Horses, and a meal was eaten.

VIII

"Across Indian Territory,
Through the heart of Choctaw country,
Rolled the stagecoach. Ormsby noted
His surprise at finding Indians
Managing the line's home stations,
Where meals were served to passengers.
Choctaws also were employed
At swing stations, where the horses
Were exchanged and pastured, stabled.
Members of a Civilized Tribe,
The Choctaws were thrifty farmers.

"After crossing wide Red River
On a ferry operated
By another Choctaw, the stage
Entered Texas where the Indians
Were no longer friendly. Drivers
And the other stage attendants
Checked their guns and kept them handy.

IX

"On the northern fringe of Texas
Ormsby saw a few white settlers.
But the land soon changed to virgin
Landscapes with no hint of home sites.

"On past Belknap and the tumbled
Ghostly ruins of old Fort Phantom
Where there was no change of horses—
The Comanches had been active—
Sped the stagecoach toward Fort Chadbourne.

"When they crossed the Concho River,
They were on one of the stretches
Where stations were not completed:
Here a herd of mules was driven
On ahead to provide changes.

"After passing Horsehead Crossing,
Dashing toward the Guadalupes,
Roads improved and Ormsby stated
That the grandeur of the scenery
Was beyond words of description.

"Nearly a hundred miles east of
El Paso, a curt command of
'Halt!' accompanied by gunfire
Rent the air, and Ormsby peered out
To see a stagecoach approaching.

"The command to halt was greeting
Of outriders of the eastbound
Stage, which had left California
On the fourteenth of September.

Both stagecoaches were ahead of
Schedule, so they took a moment
To celebrate and agree that
'Nothing must stop the U. S. Mail,'
Motto of the new stage service.

" 'Here the East meets West,' said Bailey,
Who was representative of
Brown, the postmaster general,
And riding the eastbound stagecoach.

X

"Whips cracked and the coaches started
With a lurch toward destinations.
Drivers were intent on living
Up to lofty expectations
Of John Butterfield, their daring
Boss, who with undaunted courage,
Tackled a job that people said
Could not be done — they would show them!

"Interest of the people mounted.
Bets were placed and odds were given
That John Butterfield's great venture
Would go down in utter failure.

"But the people failed to reckon
With the grim determination
Of the Butterfield employees,
All of whom were wisely chosen.
Drivers performed many worthy
Feats of courage and endurance.

"Their enthusiasm seemed to
Be contagious, spread to horses—
Pegasus could not have beaten
Them as they raced over prairies,
Mountains, deserts, rises, lowlands . . .
Speed and daring seemed to become
Watchwords of the drivers, horses.

XI

"Ormsby's stage was fast approaching
Country of the fell Apaches—
Land of Cochise, wise old warrior
Who is chief of Chiricahuas.

"Ormsby, talking with the driver,
Said that he had heard that Cochise
Was the fiercest Indian chieftain
In all of the desert country.

" 'That is surely right,' the driver
Answered, 'but he is an able
And, some say, sagacious leader.'
"In a treaty made with major
Stein he granted a safe passage
To all white men through his domain.
He appears to be trustworthy.
More than two years have elapsed since
He made peace, and he has kept it.
I believe he will continue
To be faithful to the treaty,
That is, unless some fool white man
Doublecrosses Chiricahuas.

"As they talked the huge vehicle
Whirled onward toward the sunset.
When the moon came up it witnessed
A new scene, a stagecoach streaking
Through the desert night — a vision
It was destined to see often.

"Dragoon Springs was the next station.
Soon they thundered on toward Tucson,
Ancient town of dun adobe
Houses and a Spanish mission.
On beyond the Colorado
River, which they crossed by ferry,
They dipped south across the border
To avoid the burning desert.

XII

"As they entered California,
They ran into Indian trouble.
A small band of mounted red men
Blocked the road beside the station.
They announced that they proposed to
Put an end to stagecoach travel.

"The conductor and the driver
Grabbed their rifles as the station
Crew ran out and started firing.
Indians, armed with bows and arrows
And a few old muzzle loaders,
Soon retreated, cowed and beaten.

XV

"With Los Angeles behind them,
They were back in civilization.

When the stage reached San Francisco,
On the tenth day of October,
A full day and thirty minutes
Ahead of the 'hopeless' schedule,
San Franciscans celebrated.
It was hard to realize that
They were getting mail from eastern
Cities faster than the fastest
Steamship ever had delivered
It, and many weeks ahead of
The old intermittent service
That had come through Salt Lake City.
Years of pleading were rewarded—
Washington had heard and answered!

XIV

"Ormsby was the featured speaker
At a gala celebration
Held in Music Hall. The firing
Of a thirty-two gun salute
Was typical of proportions
Of the city's all-out effort
To express appreciation
To John Butterfield for doing
The impossible — connecting
East and West with fast mail service.

"And the line is benefitting
Us and all the other people

On the route the stages travel.
Rapid means of transportation
Coupled with communication
Will do much to build this country."

XV

Bitsy, half asleep when Newton
Finished his exciting story,
Nodded, "You are sure right, Daddy,
They help . . . and I like stagecoaches."
Newton kissed her as he promised:
"I will take you to the stage road
One of these days so that you may
See the stagecoach pass. You'll like that!"

"It will not be necessary,"
Little Newton explained slowly.
"We were there today!" His daddy
Listened as he told the story
Of their ride to see the stagecoach.

"Thank you, Son, for telling Daddy,
But do not forget your promise.
It is dangerous to wander
Beyond sight of those who love you.
One day we will ride the stagecoach
All the way to San Francisco.
Now be off to bed . . . both of you!"

Chapter Thirty-four

The Changing Scene

IT WAS AUGUST when Lucinda
Gave birth to her third child, a son,
Malcolm, named for Colonel Lovelace.
Little Newton and Miss Bitsy
Were delighted with their brother.
Newton and Lucinda's boundless
Happiness was sharp-reflected
In each tender glance and caress.

Gently rocking Malcolm's cradle
On a bright September morning,
Newton was beset by coughing.

"Newton, dearest," asked Lucinda,
Have you talked with Doctor Wilson?
Your cough has me deeply worried."

"It is nothing," Newton answered.
"But if it will make you happy,
I will see the doc tomorrow
When I go for patrol duty."

II

Following examination,
Doctor Wilson stated firmly:
"Symptoms indicate consumption,
But I cannot be full certain
Until tests have been completed.
You should enter the hospital
While I check out your condition."

"That's impossible," said Newton,
There's Comanche trouble brewing
East of here, and I have orders
To investigate. We leave here
Just as soon as a contingent
Can be readied. I will be back
In a few days and will see you . . . "

"I still say," said Doctor Wilson,
"You should be in the hospital.
I insist that you contact me
When your mission is completed."

"I will do that," Newton promised,
"But this is a temporary
Ailment that will clear up shortly."

"I hope you are right," the doctor
Said, "but I am very fearful
That you are, indeed, mistaken."

III

The reconnaissance continued
For a month and Newton's coughing

Spells grew worse. He started losing
Weight. Inertia overtook him.

Worried, Sergeant Beaman summoned
A conveyance to transport him
Back to Cooper. Doctor Wilson,
In emergency, had been sent
To Fort Chadbourne to assist with
An outbreak of typhoid fever.

IV

Somewhat rested, Newton ordered
Driver of the ambulance to
Take him to the ranch. Lucinda
Greatly distressed, quickly doctored
Him with remedies at hand, and
He responded in a manner
That surprised them all. "The Indians,"
He said in a talk with Edwin,
"Seem determined to recapture
All of huge *Comancheria*.
Many settlers are already
Moving back to eastern regions
Where they will be safe till problems
Can be permanently settled."

V

"What has caused this change? Lucinda
Asked. "Once peaceful Clear Fork Valley,
With exception of Camp Cooper,
Has in ninety days reverted
To the dread *Comancheria*.

Resurrected Indian troubles
Are a repititious nighmare."

Newton thoughtfully responded:
"When we first came to the valley
It was undisturbed by settlers.
Edwin's friendship with the chieftain
Pah-hah-yo-ko helped to cement
Good relations with Comanches.

"Locating the reservation
Here was also influential
In preserving peace. Comanches
Watched experiments in hope that
A solution might develop
To their sad vexatious problems.

"But impatient and imprudent
Actions of the Indian-haters
In the war on reservations
Were unwarranted and only
Served to jeopardize the safety
Of all settlers in the outlands.

"The decision for removal
Of the Indians had been ordered
Before violence erupted.

"It is natural that wild tribes
Would avenge the foul abuses
Of their brothers who were willing
To assist in what seemed futile
Efforts to solve hopeless problems.

"Now the pendulum is swinging
Back and forth between the red men

Fighting to retain their homelands
And frontiersmen pushing westward.

"There will come a time when Indians
Roam no more the lands of Texas . . .
It will not come in the twinkling
Of an eye, but it is dawning
Just as surely as tomorrow
Even now is in the making.

 "With the slavery situation
Crowding out all other issues,
It seems evident that white men
Soon will war with one another.

"When that day arrives — tomorrow,
Next week, or next year — the soldiers
Stationed at the border outposts
Will be called to active duty
In a war that overshadows
Interest in Indian troubles.

"When the military withdraws,
Indians will again take over . . .
For that reason it were better,
Edwin, that you take the livestock
Back to Indian Territory
Until redskin raids are over.

"David, Ramon, and Conchita
Will remain here with Lucinda
And the children while I journey
To San Antonio for treatment."

VI

It was warm for late October,
And at eventide Lucinda
Said, "I'd like to watch the sunset.
Let us walk out by the spring-house."

As the flaming orb descended,
Salmon, saffron, red, and turquoise
Banners waved over castellated
Battlements of buttes and mesas,
Strewn like citadels long-toppled
On the bosom of the prairie.

Newton gently took Lucinda's
Hand and led her to a grassy
Seat beside the gushing springlet.
In her ear he softly whispered:
"This is paradise . . . The Garden:
Gaze upon the master painting
Of the valley's gorgeous sunset—
'Tis ethereal, enthralling!

"Hear the symphony of limpid
Waters tumbling toward the Clear Fork.
No cathedral organ ever
Played such music. The sublime notes
Flowing from the stone keys chiseled
By the rushing, crystal springlet
Are like those of sweet angelic
Harpists in the choir of Heaven!"

"You are right, dear," said Lucinda.
I am sure that Eden's garden

Was in no respect more perfect
Than this mild October evening
In the Valley of the Clear Fork."

When the moon was high above them,
Newton broke the spell and whispered:
"Morpheus awaits us, darling . . .
Besides, I take Little Newton
On a hunting trip tomorrow."

Fearfully, Lucinda shuddered,
But she did not raise objection.

Walking toward the house they halted
To admire the startling beauty
Of the scene outspread before them:
Stone Ranch and its mute surroundings,
Shimmering in light and shadow,
Formed a medieval castle
Buttressed to a wall of moonbeams.

VII

"How would you like to go hunting?"
Newton asked his son next morning.

In glee, Little Newton answered,
"Daddy, that's a silly question.
You know I am always ready
For a hunt. Let me call Billy."

Billy Spivens was a friendly
Hound that took to Little Newton
Like a mallard takes to water,
Boy and dog were fast companions.

All day long the hunt continued
At a pace that was not tiring.
They observed much game, but Newton
Killed just what he thought sufficient
For their needs, some quails and squirrels.

When the evening shadows lengthened,
They made camp in open country
Bordering a strip of woodland.
Newton took the axe and started
After wood. "Son," he instructed,
"You walk over to that thicket,"
Pointing to a nearby plum grove,
"Get some dry twigs for a starter.
We will have a fire in no time."

VIII

As the boy approached the thicket
He could hear a late-fall rattler,
Looked and saw the huge snake coiling
Just beyond its striking distance.

Little Newton froze and whistled.
Billy Spivens bounded forward.
Baying hound and buzzing rattler
Engaged in a fearsome battle
That would mean death to the loser.
Billy Spivens lunged; the rattler
Struck forcefully, gold fangs shining
In the fading rays of sunlight.
But it missed, and Billy Spivens
Grabbed it, biting, chewing, shaking,
All in one unerring motion.

When he turned it loose, the rattler,
Writhing, squirming in convulsions,
Turned its cold pale belly skyward.

Newton, noting the commotion,
Dropped his wood and hurried over
Just in time to see Bill Spivens
End the deadly, gruelling duel.

"That was a close call," said Newton.

"Yes, sir, close!" the boy responded.

Newton slapped him on the buttock,
Smiled, but inwardly he trembled.

After supper they sat talking
By the fire. A fit of coughing,
Uncontrollable, exhausting,
Wracked the frame of Newton Givens.

Frightened, Little Newton asked him:
"Dad, can I do something for you?"
"No Son," Newton shrugged in answer,
"I will be fine in a minute."
Soon he was relaxed, and Little
Newton said in admiration:
"Dad, I'm sure you know, but I want
To express appreciation
For the hunts we've had together.
Nothing makes me happier than
Being with you when we're hunting!"

IX

"Thank you, Son," said Newton smiling,
"But I want you to remember

There's a great deal more to hunting
Than just thrilling to the baying
Of the hounds and killing quarry:
There are big wide open spaces,
Broken hills and narrow canyons,
Rugged, beautiful, and waiting
Eagerly to share their treasures . . .

"There is breakfast at the cracking
Of the dawn; the smell of coffee
Blended with inviting odors
Of the bacon as it sizzles
Over coals of green sweet-scented
Oak, mesquite, or honey locust . . .
There is leaning in the saddle
Of your mount when in a hurry
To catch up when dogs are treeing . . .
When the fresh wind rushes past you,
It is soothing as it whispers
That the happy chase is ending
And the trophy waits your claiming . . .

"When the dusk is tucking daylight
Into waiting arms of darkness,
And you watch the bull bats weaving
Through the sky in search of supper,
And the chirrup of a night bird
Blends with whippoorwill's announcement
That a perfect day is ending,
You look gratefully toward heaven
And thank God for all His blessings.

"There are tingling thrills in watching
Golden hunting moons probe deeply

Into mystery-laden nighttime
When the high hills in the distance
Kiss the stars in fond affection.

"When the campfire's glow is fading,
It is pleasant to remember
All the joy that goes with hunting . . .
And when sleep begins to nudge you,
You look forward to tomorrow
And to new joys that await you."

Here another spell of coughing
Shook his torture-burdened body,
Leaving Newton spent and weary.

After resting, he continued
Talking to his son in quiet
Tones: "My boy, when we return home,
I am going on a journey
To San Antonio. Your mother
Will need help in Edwin's absence.

"On you will fall all the duties
Of the ranch . . . and they are many . . .
But I know that you can handle
Them and keep things in good order.

"Pay your mother strict attention . . .
Comfort her while I'm away, Son."

"Yes, sir," Little Newton answered.

. . . From the bedroll close beside him
Came a gentle snore, and Newton
Knew his son was deep in slumber.

Chapter Thirty-five

Dividing Trails

TUESDAY MORNING Sergeant Beeman
Called to see how things were going
At the ranch. In conversation
He revealed that Doctor Wilson
Was back on the job from Chadbourne.

In the afternoon Lucinda
Called to David and instructed
Him to get the carriage ready.
"We are going to Camp Cooper.
I must visit with the doctor.

"Keep a close eye on Miss Bitsy,
And do not let Little Newton
Go outside before our return,"
She told Ramon and Conchita.
"I will take the baby with me."

II

"Stop the horses just a moment,"
Said Lucinda on an impulse,
When they came to desolated
Buildings of the reservation.

Climbing down she hurried over
To the old administration
Building, gazed about in wonder . . .

"The Comanche Reservation,"
Sighed Lucinda, gazing sadly
At the silent, gaping structures,
"Has become a ghastly ghostland
Where the bitter hate and anger,
Lust, and greed, and sore vexations
Of humanity in turmoil
Linger in deserted buildings
And spill out across the prairies.

"Aye, the reservation is an
Empty stage where wisps and whispers
Of the past re-enact dramas
Of a once proud race of red men
Who could not survive the hunger
Of the white man for their birthright . . .

"It is somehow reminiscent
Of Isaiah prophecying
That the 'cormorant and bittern
Shall possess it . . . the owl also . . .
And the satyr . . . and the raven . . . ' "

Climbing back into the carriage,
They drove onward toward Camp Cooper.

III

"Won't you please come in, Lucinda?"
Greeted Doctor Wilson, bowing.

"Thank you, Doctor," said Lucinda.
"I have come to make inquiry
About Newton's health. Please tell me
All you know of his condition."

"I regret," said Doctor Wilson,
"That there is no gentle manner
Of relating information
Of this type; it is the feature
I hate most in my profession:
He has 'galloping' consumption,
Probably in final stages."

"No, it cannot be!" Lucinda
Gasped. "How can you be so certain?"

"Just this morning," said the doctor,
"I completed tests I started
Before going to Fort Chadbourne."

Thoughtfully, Lucinda answered:
"Doctor, Newton never really
Seemed too ill until his final
Scouting tour, and even after
His collapse he rallied quickly.
He was hopeful that recovery
Would come quickly with the treatment
Prescribed in San Antonio."

"*Hope,*" explained the troubled doctor,
"Is characteristic of the
Disease . . . Lucinda, consumption
Is insidious. First symptons,
Often wholly disregarded,
Sometimes disappear entirely.

"It is likewise true that often
Those affected are unwilling
To believe they have consumption
Until it is so far advanced
That all medicine can do is
Ease the pain while they are dying.

"I had planned to come tomorrow
To the ranch and tell you all this,
And to urge you to hasten to
San Antonio to see him.

"You can never know, Lucinda,
How it hurts me to inform you
Of the facts . . . You had to know them."

"Yes," Lucinda sobbed, "and thank you.
Will you help me to my carriage?"

IV

"Just a moment," Doctor Wilson
Said. "I know the shock is dreadful,
But you must make preparations
For the journey . . . Let me help you.

"Now with travel so uncertain,
I suggest you send the older
Children to New Orleans on the the
Stagecoach. As you know, most soldiers
Are on constant patrol duty,
But I can arrange an escort
To San Antonio for you
And the others of your household . . .
Let me know when you are ready."

"I can let you know," Lucinda
Said, "right now. At noon tomorrow . . . "

"The escort will be there," Doctor
Wilson said. "I will be with it
To bring Bitsy and Young Newton
Here where they can catch the stagecoach
When it goes through Thursday morning.
Now I'll see you to your carriage."

V

"David," said Lucinda, gravely,
As the horses pointed ranchward:
"I have reached the end of living . . . "

She related Doctor Wilson's
Report to the weeping black man.

"We will leave at noon tomorrow
For his bedside . . . God," she murmured,
"Do not let him go without me . . . "

"Don'cha wurry, Miz Lucinda,"
Said the broken-hearted David,
"Massa will be waitin' fur yuh . . . "

VI

They descended from the carriage
In the ranch yard as war-whooping
Pah-hah-yo-ko and his warriors
Came to reclaim Clear Fork Valley.

Stunned and startled, David swiftly
Pushed Lucinda and the baby
Toward protection of the carriage,

And away from savage cross fire.

Suddenly the horses bolted,
Leaving David and Lucinda
With the baby fully exposed.

Inside, Ramon and Conchita
Kept a constant rain of bullets
Pouring into the attackers.
Little Newton and Miss Bitsy
Loaded rifles, pistols, shotguns.

VII

David took dead aim and emptied
His pistol into the chieftain.
Pah-hah-yo-ko caught a bullet
In the heart. The other warriors,
Seeing he was dead, retreated.
As they fled, they hurled their lances
At Lucinda and the baby.
David flung his giant body
As a shield before Lucinda;
Lances pierced his bulging shoulders,
And an arrow found the neck of
Wildly wailing Baby Malcolm.

When loud-whooping warriors faded
Past the empty cattle corral,
Ramon bounded from the ranch house
To assist the fallen David;
And Lucinda, shocked and pale-faced,
Gained protection of the quarters.

David's peppered shoulders spurted
Blood as lances were extracted;

382

Ramon staunched the flow. Conchita
Took the baby from Lucinda,
And a piercing moan of horror
Sounded as the almost severed
Head of Baby Malcolm wobbled
In a grisly, grotesque manner . . .
He was dead. Dry-eyed, Lucinda
Placed him in her arms and carried
Him into her room. Conchita,
Sobered, helped Ramon with David.
Through the night they strove to ease him,
And by morning he seemed better.

VIII

It was sunrise when Lucinda
Called them to her side and pointed
To the doll-like form reposing
In the inlaid jewel casket
Newton brought from far Calcutta.

Solemnly, Ramon was told to
"Dig a grave upon the summit.
When it's finished, come and get me.
I will wait here with Conchita."

When Ramon returned, Lucinda
Labored slowly up the summit . . .

IX

Elegy

. . . On a high hill overlooking
Old Stone Ranch, a cemetery
With a single grave stands vigil

Over sweeping, rugged grandeur
Of a land now roamed by cattle.

The discovery, inadvertent,
Of the tomb was made by persons
Looking for long-buried treasure.
In the tiny hand-hewn casket
Was the body of an infant.

Rocks and hills hold fast the secrect
Of the tender hands that placed it
In the hallowed earth to slumber.

Yet, to one's imagination
Comes the vision of a woman,
Bowed in grief by her bereavement,
Raising tear-dimmed eyes to heaven,
Asking God to grant her surcease
From the sorrow in her bosom . . .

Slowly bows her head in reverence;
Measured, muted words are uttered:

"Innocence and love are buried
In this grave upon the summit.
Lord, I pray for understanding
In this hour of grief and sadness . . . "

Softly then from out the silence,
Borne on gently soothing zephyr,
Floated reassuring knowledge:
"Innocence and love are risen;
Never was a tomb to hold them.
Death is but a door that opens
Into time and peace eternal . . .

In the death and resurrection
Of My own Son lies the answer:
Just as dust to dust returneth,
So does spirit unto spirit—
From the first 'twas everlasting.
Life and death are my creation;
One doth complement the other:
Go in peace, O precious mother . . . "

X

It was high noon when the escort
Reached the ranch, and Doctor Wilson
Learned of the attack. He stated:
"Pah-hah-yo-ko has been raiding
Many ranches to the eastward.
He successfully evaded
All patrols sent out to capture
Him and his bold band of warriors.

"It was fortunate that David
Killed him. It will end the grisly
Massacres he perpetrated . . .
But the cost was beyond measure.
To the list of all the other
Lives he's taken, I'm afraid that
David's name will soon be added.
I will take him to Camp Cooper
And do all I can to save him,
But the loss of blood he suffered
And the chance of complications
Make recovery most doubtful."

He told members of the escort
To place David in the wagon
He had brought in lieu of other
Transportation for the children.

Quick farewells were said as Sergeant
Beeman headed up the escort,
And the little party started
Southward, waving to the others
Who were going toward Camp Cooper.

. . . San Antonio was reached in
Record time, without incident.

XII

At the big army hospital
The doctor informed Lucinda
That Newton anticipated
Her arrival . . . "Intuition,"
Said the doctor . . . "And he knows that
He is dying . . . You may see him . . . "

XIII

"Ah, I knew you'd come, Lucinda . . .
It is wonderful to see you,
And to say once more I love you
With a love that has grown stronger
Every day since first I met you . . .

Though the golden thread is parting
For a time, do not be saddened . . .

It will only be a fleeting
Moment till we're reunited . . .
"I will wait just where the trail turns
Eastward toward the bursting sunrise . . .
Hand in hand we'll stroll together
Through the portal of the greatest
Of adventures . . . *The Forever.*

Until then . . . my dear . . . Lucinda . . . "

Closed the steel blue eyes and Newton's
Soul returned unto its Maker.

At the moment of his passing,
Far away across the plainsland,
Doctor Wilson heard the mumbled
Final words of faithful David:
"Ah is comin,' Massa Newton,"
And a smile enwrapped his features,
As he closed his eyes in slumber.

Bibliography

BOOKS

Anderson, Mabel Washburn. The Life of Stand Watie (Pryor, Oklahoma) 1915.

Adams, Andy. The Outlet (New York) 1905.

Biggers, Don H. Shackelford County Sketches (Albany, Texas) 1908.

Bristow, Joseph Quayle, LLB. Tales of Old Fort Gibson (New York) 1961.

Conkling, Roscoe P. and Margaret B. The Butterfield Overland Mail, 3 Vols., (Glendale, California) 1947.

Cook, James H. Fifty Years on the Old Frontier (Norman, Oklahoma) 1961.

DeShields, James T. Cynthia Ann Parker (St. Louis, Mo.) 1886.

Dobie, J. Frank. The Longhorns (Boston) 1941.

————. The Mustangs (Boston) 1952.

————. Editor: Adventures on Red River (Norman, Oklahoma) 1937.

Foreman, Grant. Marcy and the Gold Seekers (Norman, Oklahoma, University of Oklahoma Press) 1939.

Gard, Wayne. The Chisholm Trail (Norman, Oklahoma) 1954.

Glisan. L. Journal of Army Life (San Francisco) 1874.

Grant, Ben O. The Early History of Shackelford County (M.A. Thesis, Robert Nail Library, Albany, ms.,) 1936.

Hunter, J. Marvin. Editor, The Trail Drivers of Texas (San Antonio) 1920.

Lavender, David. Bent's Fort (New York) 1954.

Marcy, Randolph. Marcy Report: Explorations of Red River (Senate Document, Washington, D. C.) 1853.

————. Thirty Years of Army Life on the Border (New York, 1855.

DATE DUE
